The Survival

Kab

THE BRADT MINI GUIDE

Dominic Medley
Jude Barrand

Bradt Travel Guides Ltd, UK
The Globe Pequot Press Inc, USA

First published in 2003 by
Bradt Travel Guides Ltd, 19 High Street, Chalfont St Peter, Bucks SL9 9QE, England
Published in the USA by The Globe Pequot Press Inc, 246 Goose Lane, PO Box 480,
Guilford, Connecticut 06437-0480

British Library Cataloguing in Publication Data
A catalogue record for this book is available from the British Library

ISBN 1 84162 085 8

Front cover Christian Quick   *Cartoon* Jonathan Pugh   *Maps* Steve Munns

Typeset from the author's disc by Wakewing
Printed and bound in Italy by Legoprint SpA, Trento

The authors are two friends who met for the first time in Islamabad through a mutual friend and BBC journalist, Alice Coulter: 'my friend is out there, you must meet her'. Through the crazy days of endless work in Kabul the fun project of *The Survival Guide to Kabul* kept them sane. Thanks Alice.

Jude Barrand worked in Afghanistan in 2002 and 2003 for Caritas Internationalis as Press Officer. Jude is a former newspaper journalist in the west of England who moved on to Euronews in France and presenting on ITN in London. When she's abroad she also reports for Vatican Radio on current events and the work of Catholic humanitarian projects. Jude lives in Rome and has also contributed material to Fodor's *Guide to Rome*.

Dominic Medley worked in Afghanistan in 2002 for Internews as Project Director, setting up a journalist-training project from scratch. He returned in 2003 to complete this version of the guide and then worked with Radio Free Afghanistan as Project Co-ordinator and journalist trainer. He has worked in Bosnia-Herzegovina, Russia, Albania, Romania and Indonesia on media-development projects. Dominic is a former BBC journalist who reported for TV and radio in the west of England, making numerous reporting trips to Sierra Leone and Eritrea, and to Bosnia and Croatia during the conflicts as a journalist and humanitarian-aid driver. Dominic spends as much time as he can at his home in Cape Town.

ORGANISATIONS THE AUTHORS WORKED FOR IN AFGHANISTAN
Jude Barrand
Caritas Internationalis (web: www.caritas-network-for-afghanistan.org) is a confederation of 154 Catholic relief, development and social service organisations present in 198 countries and territories. Its mandate is to answer the needs of poor and vulnerable people wherever they may be regardless of faith, race or sex. Today there are four national Caritas organisations working together in Afghanistan. They are Caritas USA, known as CRS, Caritas Holland, known as Cordaid, Caritas Ireland, known as Trocaire and Caritas Germany. Caritas is committed to life-saving activities, (emergency relief), stabilising communities (assistance for basic needs, building schools, homes, clinics, irrigation schemes, digging wells, helping farmers with their agricultural needs etc) and promoting tolerance and peace.

Dominic Medley
Internews (web: www.internews.org) supports open media worldwide. In Afghanistan, the Internews project, funded by USAID, trains journalists and gives radio stations equipment. Internews has donated equipment to and trained journalists from all 14 regional radio stations as well as Radio Afghanistan, Bakhtar Information Agency, Kabul University Journalism Faculty and other media groups. Internews fosters independent media in emerging democracies, helps local groups work for the adoption of open broadcasting, telecommunications and internet

policy, produces innovative television and radio programming as well as internet content, and uses mass media to help reduce conflict within and between countries.

Radio Free Europe/Radio Liberty (web: www.rferl.org) restarted the Radio Free Afghanistan service in early 2002 broadcasting in Dari and Pashto. A year later, with funding from the US Congress, RFE/RL launched a training programme for Afghan journalists. In the initial programme in 2003 24 radio journalists will receive basic training, 12 of them will progress to more advanced training and nine will receive two months of training in the US. RFE/RL is based in Prague.

FEEDBACK REQUEST

The situation in Kabul is changing rapidly and every day there is something new in the city. No guidebook could claim to keep up to date anywhere in the world and certainly not in Afghanistan. So we're aware the guide is by no means complete. Everyone in Kabul has their favourite places to visit and best places for food. We've just managed to include the popular haunts, the places we know about and have been told about. Please do send us your comments and suggestions for future editions of *The Bradt Mini Guide: Kabul* (email: info@kabulguide.net). In the meantime all updates will be placed online at www.kabulguide.net.

Contents

VII

Contents

PUBLISHER'S INTRODUCTION
Hilary Bradt

We pride ourselves on our ability to act fast, but even we excelled ourselves with this unique guide. From the moment the proposal arrived on my desk in January 2003 we were interested, but when we learned that the original version was sold on the streets of Kabul by destitute children we knew we must publish it if we could – providing that street kids could continue to sell it. It's not often that the chance to 'give something back' is so immediate and easy to achieve.

Bradt has been in the forefront of responsible travel since our early guides of the 1970s, but 'giving something back' through our guidebooks has been a more recent concept, stemming from my own experience of aiding a charity in Madagascar that helps street children. I have learned a great deal about the resourcefulness of street kids and how relentlessly tough their lives are. If this mini guide to Kabul can continue the fantastic work started by Dominic and Jude with their *Survival Guide to Kabul*, we will be satisfied. If it helps those who are working with the Afghan people to rebuild their lives it will have achieved a double purpose. And if it gives readers in the Western world a greater understanding of the challenges that face the people of Afghanistan, we will have achieved what we all set out to do.

Where would we be without the support of our colleagues and friends? Without a doubt, we'd still be scratching around at the drawing board.

Since the first edition of the 16-page pamphlet was sold out by the street kids (big thanks to them) we could only progress to a Bradt Travel Guide with the help, advice and contributions from so many in and outside Kabul.

Thanks go to Caritas Internationalis in Rome, in particular to the Head of Communications Lynn Yuill for her encouragement. Thanks also to the Caritas office in Kabul and the boundless enthusiasm of Caritas programme advisor François Large. When he wasn't searching for new ways of getting Afghanistan back on its feet, he was offering invaluable support and advice to the authors. His constant scouting for new places to visit have made the guide a far richer project than it would ever have been without him.

Thanks to Caritas programme advisors, Salima Padamsey and LeAnn Hager, for being such dynamic sources of inspiration and good friends and to Brian O'Callaghan who proofread the first edition, offered encouragement and weeded out the grammatical errors and spelling mistakes.

Thanks to Internews who gave Dominic the chance to come to Afghanistan. He then discovered his great-great grandfather marched from Kabul to Kandahar with General Lord Roberts.

In 2002 Sanjar Qiam, the Internews Assistant, made a thousand little chores and errands melt away thanks to his efficient time management and contacts and in 2003 his brother Massoud helped us out. The Internews Assistant in Islamabad,

Acknowledgements

Saleh Shaikh, ensured the 2,000 pamphlets and 1,000 cups and pens were printed and delivered to Kabul.

The contribution of two superb journalists helped the project enormously. Ahmed Rashid's generous contribution of an exclusive article for the first edition helped make the guide an instant hit. Eddie Girardet's advice about what to include helped us immeasurably as well.

Particular thanks to the Afghanistan Information Management Service, AIMS (web: www.aims.org.pk) for permission to use the map of Kabul in the street edition of the guide in autumn 2002 and to use their maps of Kabul for the basis of the maps in this guide.

We are also indebted to those first pioneers who brought chocolate mud pie and carrot cake to Kabul. Our thanks go to Matt Woods from Bs Place for the warmth and comfort of home cooking and to Wais Faizi of the Mustafa Hotel for all his round-the-clock availability and advice about Kabul and tips on where to go. The Gandamak Lodge provided us with a safe haven.

Thank you to all those people and organisations that sent us suggestions and emails to ensure they were mentioned in the guide. Keep them coming please.

Thanks to Bradt Travel Guides. They were the first to ring out of 25 publishers we approached.

Finally, a big thank you and best wishes to the welcoming people of Kabul at all the restaurants, hotels, guesthouses, historical sites and on the streets. We, too, hope life has changed for the better in your amazing city.

Acknowledgements

This guidebook has humble beginnings during the early months of chaos, renewed international interest and the start of reconstruction in Afghanistan. In the summer of 2002 we were having lunch in Kabul and realised there was no one source of information for all the new phone numbers in Kabul – the new GSM system, the satellite phones, all the old landlines and digital numbers. Added to that there were thousands of internationals arriving and millions of Afghans returning home. We soon hit on the idea of *The Survival Guide to Kabul*. We managed to bring together 16 pages of information in an A5 format. We started printing 500 copies on office printers, stapling late at night and on our Fridays off. We had 500 printed in Kabul and 2,000 more professionally printed in Islamabad.

Then came the problem of distribution. There we were helped by the city's newspaper sellers, almost all of whom are young children. Across Kabul the children sell newspapers to make money for their families. They buy the newspapers for 1 Afghani (around 2 cents), and sell them for about 10 Afghanis (approximately 20 cents), more if possible. If the papers have English pages the children approach every international stuck in the Kabul traffic and sell for the highest price. This, we realised, was the way to get the guide out. We also decided that the project should be a way of helping the children. In September after the first guides rolled off the printer, we gathered a group of youngsters and explained that we would like them to distribute our booklet. We gave them a price guide and we also told them whatever they made in selling it was all theirs. Soon we had 15–20 kids at our doors every day wanting more copies of the guide.

Introduction

The average salary in Kabul is around US$40 a month. By selling the guides for a minimum of US$1 a go the children were making good money for their needy families. They took to the venture with gusto and even established an informal union to ensure no-one undercut the market by selling the guides for less than the agreed dollar.

When the guides sold out the internet took over. The online version of the guide (now at www.kabulguide.net) continues to score thousands of hits. Embassies started printing the pages from the web. Links appeared on websites from the US Department of Commerce and the International Organisation of Migration, with its programme to encourage Afghans to return. The guide featured in a Swedish newspaper; copies were available on UN planes to Kabul; the Mustafa Hotel had the web address painted on the main walls of the hotel entrance.

And then on December 28 2002 *The Survival Guide to Kabul* featured in *The Times* of London travel section: 'Latest guidebook gossip: What's on in sunny Kabul'. The accompanying cartoon featured two travellers in sleeping bags on the street outside the Hotel Kabul. One says: 'I wouldn't complain … this room's an upgrade.'

So this guide itself is an upgrade to the pamphlet and material available online. It is designed as a pocket-sized guide so you can always have useful details and contacts at your fingertips. Finally, we will be using our street children network to make as many of the Kabul sales of this guide as possible, in the hope that it benefits them as much this time round as it did the last.

Welcome to Kabul and Afghanistan. You've arrived for 'The Great Game'. *Salaam a-laykum!*

©The Times

AFGHANISTAN AT A GLANCE

Location Southern Asia, north and west of Pakistan, east of Iran, south of Turkmenistan, Uzbekistan, Tajikistan

Size 647,500 km²

Climate Cold winters and hot summers

Time GMT +4 hours 30 minutes

International telephone code +93

Status Islamic Transitional State of Afghanistan (web: www.af)

Currency Afghani (AFA). 50 Afghanis = US$1 (approx)

Population 27,755,775 (July 2002 estimate)

Population growth per year 3.43% (2002 estimate)

Life expectancy in years at birth Male 46 years, female 45

Infant mortality 144.76 deaths/1,000 live births (2002 estimate)

Capital Kabul; population 1.5–2.5 million (2002 estimate)

Kabul GPS location 34°31'12.01"N; 69°10' 48.94"E; altitude: 1,777m

Main towns Herat, Kandahar, Jalalabad, Mazar-i-Sharif

Language Pashto, Dari and other local languages

Religion Islamic faith (Sunni Muslim 84%, Shi'a Muslim 15%)

Flag Broad black, red and green vertical bands with coat of arms in the centre band featuring temple, wreath and Arabic text

INTRODUCTION

September 11 2001 changed everything for Afghanistan and its capital city, Kabul. The terrorist attacks in New York and Washington put Afghanistan firmly on the international agenda as the US-led bombing campaign to root out Al Qaeda started.

Within just two months, on November 13, Taliban forces fled Kabul and the victorious Northern Alliance moved in. The US-led War on Terror continued around the country well into 2002 and 2003. There were assassinations and fatal bombings in Kabul and elsewhere. The situation was tense. But Afghanistan seems to have emerged from more than 23 years of constant fighting.

In Kabul change has been rapid, unbelievable and hopefully, *Inshallah* (God willing), irreversible.

The most important catalyst for change has been the fall of the repressive, prohibitive Taliban regime which has lead to a city-wide renaissance. People started watching international satellite TV, even making their own satellite dishes out of Coke and hairspray cans. Afghan TV began broadcasting again. The Cinema Park began showing Bollywood action and dancing movies. *Titanic* was seen to be too erotic by the manager, even though most teenagers in Kabul had seen it several times on video compact disc. Despite the establishment restrictions it seemed to be the most popular film in the city. Down 'Technology Street', near the Khyber Restaurant, every kind of technical item was for sale. In March 2002 one shop reported selling 300 televisions in just two days.

Across town you could buy movies on video compact disc, everything starring

Background

Arnold Schwarzenegger, Sylvester Stallone and Jean Claude Van Damme. James Bond was hugely popular; so was Mr Bean. Postcards and posters of Indian film stars were on sale in the kiosks. Photo booths reopened. The radio was openly listened to again and Indian, Afghan and Iranian music blared from cassette players in the bazaars and from every taxi.

Some women felt brave enough to slowly remove the all-encompassing blue *burqa*. Men shaved their beards off.

Huge numbers of humanitarian agencies and the United Nations re-established themselves in Kabul and embassies reopened. Thousands of Afghan refugees returned from Pakistan, Iran and around the world, especially America. By the summer of 2002, returning refugees from Pakistan were even bringing cricket to Afghanistan.

There was a genuine atmosphere of freedom and excitement in the city. Girls went back to school after five years of exclusion under the Taliban; women were employed in government ministries and international agencies; restaurants opened, a thriving guesthouse business developed and souvenir shops began a roaring trade in carpets. Stationery and computer shops opened to feed the growing international community hosting conferences and workshops.

There were numerous weddings and parties for returning Afghans with music, dancing and even alcohol.

For the authors of this guide, first-time visitors to Afghanistan in 2002, to observe the changes over a two-year period has been amazing. For those who had been watching and reporting on Afghanistan for more than 20 years there was clearly no going back to the dark, bad old days. Ordinary Afghans had been liberated and were enjoying their freedom.

GEOGRAPHY AND CLIMATE

Afghanistan is a landlocked country roughly the size of Texas. The magnificent mountain ranges make up some two thirds of the country. Rivers flow from the high mountains in the Hazarjat and the Hindu Kush; deserts stretch westwards from Kandahar.

Afghanistan has a continental climate that is spared the monsoons that affect the Indian subcontinent thanks to the high mountain range between Pakistan and Afghanistan. Summers are hot and dry and winters are harsh. There are four distinct seasons with huge variations between them. Rainfall is extremely light, less than a metre per annum; most of this rain falls in March. The rest of the water supply comes from the melting snow that caps the great mountain ranges in the centre of the country. Temperatures range from $-35°C$ in the mountainous regions in winter to $55°C$ in the southern desert region south of Kandahar in the summer. Kabul is more temperate, however, with winter lows of around $-10°C$ and summer highs of $35°C$.

Most of the country is empty desert or uninhabitable mountain ranges. Only a fraction of the land is fit for cultivation, the rest is barren. The country is currently in its fifth year of a devastating drought.

Geography and climate

THE STORY OF ONE OF THE STREET SELLERS

Orphan Naser Barotali has been selling 'The Survival Guide to Kabul'. With his income he supports his younger brother and his blind grandfather.

I was born in a district of West Kabul called Barhgre Ali Mardan in 1987. My younger brother Nasieer was born two years after me.

We grew up in a very difficult time. The different Mujaheddin commanders were fighting for control of the city and there was a lot of bombing and fighting in our area. Our lives were very hard, but then one day when I was about eight years old a large rocket exploded near our house. My father ran out to see what had happened and that was the last time we saw him alive. A gunman in the street shot him and a friend of his who had gone with him.

After that our lives became very sad and difficult. My father was no longer around to earn a living to keep us alive and my mother was devastated by grief. A year later she too died. Her death was due to a broken heart.

After that my brother and I had to fend for ourselves until my grandfather came to get us. He took us from our family home as the fighting was getting worse and the bombs were falling all around us. Together we fled to Jalalabad where we lived in a camp for displaced people. I was about eight or nine then, I can't quite remember exactly how old I was, but I remember being sad and scared.

There were thousands of people in the camp; all of them had moved to escape the fighting. By now Kabul was a death zone.

After three years in the camp in Jalalabad (I can't remember its name), one of my paternal uncles came for my brother and me and said he could find work for us at a carpet factory in Pakistan. As there was no-one in our family who could care for my brother and I, we left for Peshawar.

We lived with my uncle in Haji Camp, a community of Afghan refugees in Peshawar town, but our lives were very sad and very hard there. Every morning we would have to get up at 4am to go to work at the carpet factory. Our day would end at 9pm. Sometimes I was so tired I would fall asleep. When that happened the factory owner beat me on the head with a metal hook used for weaving the carpets. The good thing is that we were fed.

We had hot meals, rice, potatoes and meat sometimes. The factory owner would also give us his children's second-hand clothes. At least we had food. In my two years in the carpet factory I made five large carpets and my brother made 12 smaller ones. In all that time we were never once paid, as we were considered apprentices. We wanted to run away, but we didn't dare because we were told that the child snatchers would catch us and take us to a KharGhar (Forced Labour Camp) where we would never see our relatives again.

Geography and climate

My brother and I were very unhappy. The conditions in the factory were very bad. Hot in summer, cold in winter, and we were beaten. Every day we would pray for my grandfather to come and get us and take us away back to Afghanistan. Finally one of my aunts told my grandfather how miserable we were and he came and rescued us last year.

After so many years we all came home to Kabul. We live in the same district as before in West Kabul. We have no heating, water or electricity. My brother and I both work now selling newspapers and we support my grandfather who is unemployed. He is blind and cannot work. It takes me about 40 minutes every day to come to work in the city centre where I sell newspapers. Every morning I get ten newspapers from the paper seller and then at the end of the day I pay him. Usually I make 40,000–50,000 Afghanis a day (50,000 old Afghanis = US$1) then I pay him the 30,000 Afghanis (70c) for the papers.

My profit was so small we could barely survive.

Two months ago I heard that Dominic (Medley) was giving out survival guides to us street sellers. He was already a customer of mine, so I hurried

Natural disasters have played their part in Afghanistan's history. A devastating earthquake in northern Afghanistan in February 1998 killed 4,000 people and left 30,000 homeless. The Taliban regime was reluctant to allow aid workers access to

over to ask for some guides so I could sell them too. Now I get five guides a day and I sell them for between 60,000 to 70,000 Afghanis each. The good thing about the guide is that I get to keep all the profit. I use the money to buy extra food for my family. Usually I buy oil, sugar and flour.

Most days I have tea and naan (bread) for breakfast, potatoes and rice for lunch and potatoes and rice for dinner. I never usually get meat.

I cannot read or write and I have never been to school. I go to mosque, but I am illiterate. I don't know what to expect for the future. I do not think I will have an easy life. My parents are dead, my grandfather is old and my brother and I are the only ones to care for him.

I am sad for my life and sad for my future. There's no one to care for us. My life is just standing and selling newspapers. My future is bad.

The money I get from selling the newspaper is not enough, so I am happy to sell the guide and Dominic is the best guy in Kabul. I don't know if he is the best guy in Afghanistan because I don't know the other provinces, but I can say he's the best in Kabul.

the region. A further quake in May of the same year killed more than 5,000 people. And in early 2002 a series of earthquakes in the Hindu Kush killed thousands of people with tremors of several minutes being felt in Kabul.

Geography and climate

A MOGUL'S WORD ON KABUL'S CLIMATE

The Mogul Emperor Babur, who conquered Kabul in 1504, grew to love the city. His descriptions of the place that became his adopted home are with us still, and they hold true today. He dwells at length on its ideal location and climate in his memoirs, *The Baburnama*.

[Kabul] is situated in an exceptionally elevated place with wonderfully good air. It overlooks the large lake and three meadows which when green make a beautiful sight. In the spring and summer in Kabul the north-wind, which they call the Parwan Wind, never dies down...nearby are regions with both warm and cold climates. Within a day's ride from Kabul it is possible to reach a place where snow never falls. But within two hours one can go where the snows never melts.

NATURAL HISTORY AND CONSERVATION

Landmines and unexploded ordinance cover much of Afghanistan. Destroyed tanks, airplanes and military hardware litter the country – there are more than 120 burnt-out tanks lining the roadside between Kabul and Bamyian. Four years of drought has devastated agriculture, and forests in some areas have been reduced by 50% since 1978.

Background

A United Nations Environmental Programme (UNEP) assessment in late 2002 called for environmental restoration to play a major part in reconstruction efforts. UNEP Executive Director Klaus Toepfer said: 'Over 80% of Afghan people live in rural areas, yet they have seen many of their basic resources – water for irrigation, trees for food and fuel – lost in just a generation. In urban areas the most basic necessity for human well being – safe water – may be reaching as few as 12% of the people.'

The water table has lowered, and noticeably so in Kabul, with many people drilling deeper wells in the summer of 2002 and having to use generators all day as water in the hydro-electric dam was low. The UNEP found that the damaged water system in Kabul is lacking routine maintenance and is losing up to 60% of its supply through leaks and illegal use.

Huge tracts of forest have been sold off by warlords, mainly to Pakistan, and deforestation is a serious problem that is also raising the spectre of soil erosion.

Wildlife too has suffered over the years from hunting. Snow leopards could number as few as a hundred and it is not rare to see their fur on sale in Chicken Street, in Kabul, for more than US$1,000.

HISTORY

Afghans will tell you that their country is historically a product and a victim of its geographic location. At the crossroads of Central Asia and as the main land route between the east and west, Afghanistan has drawn travellers, nomads, traders and warriors through its rugged terrain from time immemorial.

History

Chronology

330BC	Alexander the Great invades Afghanistan.
1219	Genghis Khan invades Afghanistan.
1504	Kabul becomes capital of Mogul Empire under Babur Shah.
1838–42	Massacre of the British Kabul garrison and start of the first Anglo-Afghan War.
1878–80	Second Anglo-Afghan War: General Lord Roberts leads army from Kabul to Kandahar on his famous forced march to avenge British military rout.
1919	Third Anglo-Afghan War and independence for Afghanistan from Britain, August 19.
1926	Amanullah proclaims himself king.
1929	Amanullah flees.
1933	Zahir Shah becomes king.
1953	General Mohammad Daud becomes prime minister.
1963	Daud is forced to resign as prime minister.
1964	A constitutional monarchy is introduced.
1973	King Zahir Shah is deposed in a coup by his cousin Mohammad Daud who declares a republic.
1978	Daud is overthrown and killed.
1979	Power struggle between leftist leaders Amin and Taraki. Amin wins but Soviet Union sends in troops (thousands land in Kabul on December 24). Amin executed.

Background

1980	Supported by Soviet troops, Babrak Karmal, leader of the People's Democratic Party, is installed as ruler.
1985	Mujaheddin alliance formed in Pakistan.
1986	Babrak Karmal is replaced by Najibullah.
1988	Geneva Peace Accords.
1989	February 15: Soviet troops leave Afghanistan.
1992	Najibullah's regime falls. Mujaheddin enter Kabul.
1993	Burhanuddin Rabbani proclaimed president.
1994	An estimated 25,000 people killed in Kabul, victims of the faction fighting.
1996	September 27: Taliban seize control of Kabul. Rabbani flees. Najibullah executed.
1997	Pakistan and Saudia Arabia recognise Taliban regime.
2001	March: Taliban blow up Bamyian Buddhas.
2001	September 9: Northern Alliance leader Ahmad Shah Massoud assassinated.
2001	September 11: attacks on Washington and New York.
2001	October: Coalition air strikes begin on Afghanistan.
2001	November 13: Taliban flee Kabul.
2001	Bonn Peace Agreement: December 22 Hamid Karzai becomes chairman of Interim Administration.
2002	Britain establishes ISAF peacekeeping force and hands control over to Turkey in June.

History

2002	June: Loya Jirga or grand assembly chooses new government. Hamid Karzai becomes president. King Zahir Shah becomes 'Father of the Nation.'
2002	September 5: Karzai escapes assassination attempt in Kandahar; 30 people die in Kabul bomb attack.
2003	Germany and Netherlands have command of ISAF. NATO will take command.

Early history

Archaeological evidence shows that the region was widely inhabited during the palaeolithic and neolithic eras. There are also signs of agriculture and pastoral activity dating from around 10,000 years ago. By 6000BC the semi-precious stone lapis lazuli from Badakhshan was being exported to India and by 2000BC lapis could be found in the Aegean area; clear indications that Afghanistan was home to a settled and productive population.

It is not until the 6th century BC that the region started to appear in recorded history as Cyrus the Great and then his successor Darius the Great expanded the Persian kingdom into India, drawing Afghanistan into their empire on their way through.

By the 4th century BC, however, Persian rule gave way to Greek as Alexander the Great embarked on his epic march to the east, subduing first Persia and then entering Afghanistan in 330BC before moving on to India. The death of Alexander the Great 13 years later marked the disintegration of his empire and the rise in Afghanistan of Indian rulers from the Mauryan dynasty.

Since then, the region has been continuously crossed over by invading forces. In AD642 Arabs invaded bringing Islam with them. The Persians took over again until 998 when Mahmud Ghazni invaded. Numerous princes tried to rule after the Mahmud dynasty until the Mongols invaded with devastating effect in 1219.

While the dates of the arrival of the Persians and Greeks in Afghanistan are known, the exact age of Kabul is not. However, it is a fact that the city was already a flourishing hub by the time Alexander the Great turned up, making Kabul at least 2,500 years old.

The Moguls

In 1219 the Mongols invaded Afghanistan led by Genghis Khan. Mass slaughter and destruction followed. Cities such as Herat, Ghazni and Balkh were rased to the ground. In 1227 Genghis Khan died. Numerous princes followed him until the late 14th century when Timur Tamerlane, a Turko-Mongol who claimed descent from Genghis Khan, brought Afghanistan into his Asian empire. In contrast to Genghis Khan's ruinous reign of terror, Timur's arrival heralded the golden Timurid era and a flourishing of the arts. Poetry, art and architecture reached new heights

At the beginning of the 16th century, Babur, a descendant of Tamerlane and the founder of India's Mogul dynasty, made Kabul his capital, putting the city on the world map as a great seat of power. The once spectacular Babur Gardens are Babur's legacy to the city and the site of his tomb.

However, once the Mogul Empire became established in India, Afghanistan was eclipsed in importance and the country's status began to wane.

History

The Durranis

Since 1747, when Ahmad Shah Durrani established his rule over Afghanistan, all of the country's leaders have been from the Durrani's Pashtun tribe. A quick glance at his achievements gives some idea why. Ahmad Shah consolidated and enlarged Afghanistan, defeating the Moguls in the west of the Indus and taking Herat away from the Persians. His territory extended from Central Asia to Delhi, from Kashmir to the Arabian Sea. Under his rule Afghanistan became the greatest Muslim empire in the second half of the 18th century.

A measure of the strength of his reign has been clearly reflected in the fact that from 1818 onwards, all Afghanistan's leaders have been members of the Durrani Mohammadzai clan, with the exception of nine months in 1929 and after the 1978 coup.

The years that followed Ahmad Shah's death in 1772 saw a succession of family dynasties within the tribe wrestle with each other for power. But in 1826 the Durrani tribesman Dost Mohammad seized the throne and declared himself Amir of Kabul.

Among the many problems he faced was repelling Sikh encroachment on the Pashtun areas east of the Khyber Pass. In 1834 Dost defeated another invading force lead by Shah Shuja, one of the pretenders to the throne. This civil war gave the Sikhs the opportunity to expand westward which in turn acted as the catalyst for the first Afghan War.

Dost sent his son, Wazir Akbar Khan, to confront the Sikh troops. The Battle of Jamrud just west of Peshawar was a victory for the Afghans. Despite the triumph,

Dost nonetheless asked the British Governor-General in India, Lord Auckland, for help in tackling the Sikh problem.

The British leapt at the chance to be involved in Afghan affairs. The civil war with Shuja had left a power vacuum in central Afghanistan. The British knew only too well that the Hindu Kush was an ideal launching pad for an invasion of India. The British were also acutely aware that Russia was expanding steadily southwards from the Caucasus.

As a condition to their help, Britain told Dost to sever his ties with Russia and demanded in addition that Dost respect the independence of Peshawar and Kandahar. In return the British hinted at brokering an agreement between the Afghans and the Sikhs. However, when Auckland refused to put the agreement in writing Dost turned to the Russians.

Britain decided Dost had reached the end of his useful life for their purposes and set about inserting a puppet leader. The choice of British figurehead fell on Shah Shuja who was restored to the Afghan throne in August 1839 backed by the British army.

The Great Game

This heavy-handed British intervention in Afghan affairs, and the undercurrents that developed as a result between Russia and Britain in the 19th century, became famously known as the Great Game. The two competing powers battled for influence and control in Central Asia as Britain tried to protect her Indian

History

Empire and Russia sought to stem the British encroachments into its sphere of influence.

Throughout the wrangling, Afghanistan was caught squarely in the middle. The result of the political fall-out was the two main Anglo-Afghan wars in 1838–42 and 1878–80.

The first war took around two years to come to a head. Deep-seated resentments over the British occupation and interference with Afghan affairs finally surfaced in November 1841. A rampaging mob over-ran the heart of Kabul's old city. British command, wrong-footed and fazed, negotiated a safe passage out of Afghanistan with Dost's son Wazir Akbar Khan. In January 1842, 4,500 troops and 12,000 camp followers left for the high mountain passes that would take them back to India. Many died from exposure and the freezing conditions. Akbar Khan's men massacred the rest as they retreated through the pass. According to the legend, only one man from the British contingent survived the debacle.

Three months later, in April, the puppet ruler Shah Shuja was assassinated.

An avenging British army marched on Kabul in September 1842 and massacred many of the insurgents, destroyed the great Kabul bazaar and rased parts of nearby Charikar and the village of Istalif (a rebel hideout) before retreating again back to India via the Khyber Pass.

In 1843 Dost Mohammad was returned to the throne.

The second Anglo-Afghan war was triggered by the arrival of an uninvited

Russian delegation in Kabul in 1878. The British, angered that they were not allowed to send a similar representation, marched on Afghanistan. Surrounded by the hostile British, the Afghan ruler, Amir Yaqub Khan, the grandson of Dost, signed a treaty agreeing to conduct all foreign affairs in accordance with British wishes.

A British delegation took up residence in the Bala Hissar Fort in Kabul, but three months later on September 3 1879 they were massacred by Afghans harbouring resentment over both their presence and the treaty that they'd signed with them. This was all the prompting Britain needed to send its army back to Kabul, this time under the command of General Roberts who marched up from Kurram in India. He proceeded to instigate a reign of terror in the city and assume supreme authority in Afghanistan. In response to this, Afghan tribesmen assembled two separate forces. In 1880 they attacked a British contingent stationed near Kandahar. Roberts immediately mobilised, marching the 324 miles through searing desert in just 23 days. The next day Roberts's troops defeated the leader of the Afghan force, Amir Yaqub's brother Sardar Ayub Khan.

The third Anglo-Afghan war began in May 1919 and led to the independence of Afghanistan on August 19 1919. This time it was the incursion of an Afghan general into British territory that acted as the catalyst for conflict. Britain responded with an aerial bombardment of Kabul and Jalalabad (one and a half tonnes of munitions rained down on Jalalabad in a single day). The Afghans were horrified and Britain, having just emerged from World War I, had little further desire to fight. A ceasefire was called in June; independence came in August.

History

The royal family

The machinations of the Great Game brought Amir Abdur Rahman to the throne. He reigned from 1880–1901 when Britain and Russia marked out Afghanistan's borders. In World War 1, with Rahman at the helm, Afghanistan opted for neutrality.

In 1919 Rahman's son, Habibullah was assassinated. Amanullah, the third son, took charge of foreign policy and launched the third Anglo-Afghan war. The treaty of Rawalpindi was signed in August 1919 and Afghan independence secured.

King Amanullah's reign from 1919 to 1929 marked a period of modernisation, but in January 1929 he was forced to abdicate after he was defeated by Bacha-i-Saqao; the reforms he supported having met opposition from religious and tribal leaders.

In October 1929 Amanullah's cousin, Prince Nadir Khan, was declared King Nadir Shah after defeating Bacha-i-Saqao. Nadir Shah's reign didn't last long; in 1933 a Kabul student assassinated him. Within hours his 19-year-old son Zahir Shah succeeded to the throne until his cousin and the former prime minister Daud deposed him in a coup whilst he was on vacation in Italy in 1973.

The wars

A Human Rights Watch report in October 2001 divided the history of Afghanistan in the last 23 years into four phases: the Saur Revolution (named after the Afghan month when the April 27 1978 Communist revolution took place) and the Soviet

Background

occupation; the Geneva Accords to the Mujaheddin civil war; the Taliban's conquest of Afghanistan; and finally the US-led military intervention into Afghanistan.

After King Zahir Shah was deposed most historians agree Afghanistan began to slip into chaos and anarchy. Following a Loya Jirga in 1977, Mohammad Daud, who had deposed his cousin the king in 1973, was elected President of the Republic of Afghanistan for six years.

Civil war erupted in 1978 and Daud was killed. The People's Democratic Party of Afghanistan (PDPA) formed a government. The PDPA was made up of two factions – the Khlaq ('masses') and Parcham ('flag'). The country started its long slide into chaos as thousands of people were executed in the countryside as part of the government's attempts to reform rural society. Further north the Soviet Union watched and in December 1979 invaded Afghanistan. President Hafizullah Amin (from the Khlaq faction) was assassinated and Babrak Karmal (a Parchami) took over.

Over the next ten years more than 100,000 Soviet troops occupied Afghanistan. Around one million people were killed in the guerrilla war and from aerial bombardments. The Cold War was fought as never before with the US, Pakistan, China, Iran and Saudi Arabia supplying money and arms.

Mohammad Najibullah replaced Karmal as PDPA leader in May 1986 and became president in November 1987. In 1988 the Geneva Accords were signed and on February 15 1989 the Soviets left Afghanistan.

But the peace agreement in Geneva did not end the fighting in Afghanistan. A civil war broke out as the Mujaheddin attempted to overthrow Najibullah. In 1992 the

History

Northern Alliance was formed, militia forces in Kabul mutinied and President Najibullah fled to the UN compound (from where he and his brother were abducted in 1996 and executed by the Taliban). On April 28 1992 Ahmad Shah Massoud (see page 24) entered Kabul. The new coalition government led by Burhanuddin Rabbani excluded Gulbuddin Hekmatyar, leader of the Hezb-e-Islami (Islamic Party) faction which was blamed for much of the destruction of Kabul during the Mujaheddin infighting in the 1990s. In retaliation, Hekmatyar launched massive rocket attacks on Kabul until February 1995.

This was the beginning of the end for Afghanistan. The indiscriminate factional fighting of the Mujaheddin leaders paved the way for the rise of the Taliban.

THE TALIBAN

The Taliban movement was started in a small village between Kandahar and Lashkahgar in 1994 by a group of Islamic students with a radical approach to interpreting Islam (Talib is the Pashto word for religious student; Taliban is the plural). But the mysterious group of youth militia claiming to be God's Students, led by Mullah Omar, didn't come to the world's attention until they were appointed later that year by the government of Pakistan to protect a convoy trying to open up a trade route between Pakistan and Central Asia.

The group – comprised of Afghans trained in religious schools in Pakistan along with former Islamic fighters, or Mujaheddin – proved effective bodyguards, driving off other Mujaheddin groups who tried to loot the convoy.

Flushed with this success, the Taliban went on to take the nearby city of Kandahar, beginning a remarkable advance which led to their capture of the capital, Kabul, in September 1996.

There, one of their first actions was to storm the UN compound housing the former Communist president, Najibullah, and execute him. His body was hung on public display in the centre of Kabul to the shock and dismay of many of the city's inhabitants.

In 1997 the Taliban took Mazar-i-Sharif only to be routed in their first-ever military setback, but by September 1998 they had taken Mazar in the north and later Bamyian in the central Hazarajat region. It was in Bamyian that one of the worst atrocities of the Taliban offensive allegedly took place. Hazara fighters had killed thousands of Taliban fighters and prisoners defending Mazar. When Hazara strongholds fell the following year, the regime massacred whole communities in revenge: possibly as many as 6,000.

By now, the Taliban had increased their sphere of control to all but the far north of the country, which was the last stronghold of the famous Lion of the Panjshir, commander Ahmad Shah Massoud.

This sweeping success was made possible in part by the early support of the local population. As ethnic Pashtuns, a large part of their support came from Afghanistan's Pashtun community, disillusioned with existing ethnic Tajik and Uzbek leaders. But it was not purely a question of ethnicity. Many ordinary Afghans, weary of the prevailing lawlessness in many parts of the country, supported the Taliban's drive to create the purest Islamic state in the world. The refusal of the Taliban to

The Taliban

deal with the existing warlords whose rivalries had caused so much killing and destruction also earned them respect.

Alarm bells started ringing, however, when the Taliban announced new draconian rules. Frivolities like television, music and cinema, which they saw as symbols of Western decadence, were banned. Their attempts to eradicate crime were reinforced by the introduction of Islamic law including public executions and amputations for murder and theft respectively. A flurry of regulations forbidding girls from going to school and women from working quickly brought them into conflict with the international community.

With 90% of the country under their control, the Taliban pressed their claims for international recognition, but to their fury only Pakistan, Saudi Arabia and the United Arab Emirates accepted them as legitimate rulers of Afghanistan. The Afghan seat at the United Nations was held by the former Afghan president Burhanuddin Rabbani throughout the Taliban regime.

A run-in in September 1997 with the European Commissioner for Humanitarian Affairs, Emma Bonino, did nothing to improve the international standing of the Taliban. Emma Bonino was arrested and her officials were beaten up by the Taliban police during their visit to a Kabul hospital. The Taliban said that the group had filmed and photographed women at a hospital. After being held for about three hours the group was released. Bonino was furious and accused the Taliban of inflicting a reign of terror on her group and the people of Afghanistan.

TALIBAN LAW

The following is a partial list of the items and activities the Taliban declared to be against the Sharia, their interpretation of Islamic law:

women working and driving	dancing
television	kite-flying
satellite-TV dishes	playing cards
movies	chessboards
photographs of people and animals	neckties
statues	lipstick
stuffed toys	nail polish
the internet	fireworks
computer discs	fashion catalogues
non-religious music	poppy crops
musical instruments	pig-fat products
cassettes	anything made with human hair

In protest at the ongoing violations of human rights, UN sanctions were imposed in October 1999. They were also intended to force the Taliban to hand over the Saudi-born militant Osama bin Laden, who was accused at the time by the United

The Taliban

AHMAD SHAH MASSOUD

Throughout Kabul you'll see posters of this famous Northern Alliance leader, the 'Lion of Panjshir'. Massoud, 48, was assassinated in Khodjabauddin, his northern headquarters on the Tajik-Afghan border, on September 9 2001, just two days before the attacks on Washington and New York. Two Arab Al Qaeda operatives posing as Moroccan TV journalists blew themselves up in a small room where Massoud was holding a meeting. Whether his death and the attacks on America were linked is the subject of much speculation. There are reports that Massoud was ready to launch a major offensive against the Taliban. Al Qaeda knew that they didn't want Massoud in a military alliance with the Americans following the suicide attacks on the US. Many believe the assassination was a pre-September 11 present from Osama bin Laden to the

States of plotting the 1998 bombings of US embassies in Kenya and Tanzania, which killed more than 250 people.

A tighter regime of sanctions was imposed in December 2000. The Taliban, however, maintained Osama bin Laden was a guest in their country, and they would not take action against him.

At their height, the Taliban force is said to have boasted 25–30,000 militia, more than 200 tanks and a dozen aircraft, all captured from the Mujaheddin groups.

Taliban. Massoud spent more than 20 years on the political and military scene of Afghanistan fighting the Soviets, other Afghan warlords and then the Taliban. He was widely regarded as a charismatic and shrewd military and political leader. But the 1990s saw him fight for Kabul with Hekmatyar, Hezbe-e Wahdat (the Islamic Unity Party) and General Abdul Rashid Dostum, Uzbek and Mazar warlord, and currently deputy defence minister. In September 1996 Massoud lost control of Kabul to the Taliban and retreated north to the Panjshir Valley. The image of Massoud as a martyr and hero is not shared by many in Kabul who remember him for ordering the shelling of large parts of the city, particularly West Kabul. Marshall Fahim, the defence minister, succeeded Massoud as leader of the Northern Alliance. A visit to Massoud's tomb at the start of the Panjshir Valley (see page 152) is well worth a visit.

The Taliban were finally ousted from power by the US-led military operation Enduring Freedom in November 2001.

POLITICS

The politics is ever changing and even seasoned observers will admit it can be confusing; there are just so many players and factions. For the purposes of this guide we look at recent changes and developments at the highest level and the

Politics

key players. A full list of government ministers is in *Appendix 3*, page 164.

The Bonn Peace Agreement in December 2001 established a transitional period of government for Afghanistan. The transitional period runs from the Loya Jirga (grand assembly) in June 2002 until elections in June 2004.

On December 22 2001, with the signing of the Bonn Agreement, Hamid Karzai was chosen as the chairman of the Afghan Interim Authority. At the end of June 2002, following the Loya Jirga, Karzai was elected as president of the Islamic Transitional Government of Afghanistan.

There have been a number of movements in the cabinet and, with political instability, further changes are likely as President Karzai strives to strike a balance among the competing powers in Afghanistan.

Transport minister Dr Abdul Rahman was assassinated at Kabul airport in February 2002. Vice-President Haji Qadir, and Jalalabad governor, was assassinated in July 2002 outside his Ministry in Kabul. Karzai himself narrowly escaped death during an assassination attempt in Kandahar on September 5 2002.

Ali Ahmad Jalali was appointed as interior minister in February 2003 (he used to work for Voice of America). Prior to Jalali, in June 2002, Taj Mohammed Wardak had replaced one of the leading figures in the Northern Alliance, Yunus Qanooni, as interior minister.

Marshall Mohammed Fahim, defence minister and successor to Ahmad Shah Massoud as leader of the Northern Alliance, is usually referred to as first vice-president. This is not a formal position and the title tends to be used by the media

he controls. When Karzai is out of the country he does appoint an acting vice-president. Whilst he may not appoint Fahim, it is clear that the real power lies with the marshall who has military control of Kabul and reportedly a huge amount of undeclared arms in the Panjshir Valley.

Much has been made of the number of Afghan-Americans and returnee exiles in the cabinet and senior positions. No fewer than five cabinet members are Afghan-Americans who have come home. The governor of the Central Bank, Karzai's chief of staff, and vice-president Armin Arsala (finance minister from December 2001 to June 2002) are all exiles from abroad.

Ashraf Ghani, finance minister since June 2002, is a former World Bank employee though it is former finance minister Armin Arsala's signature that is on the new Afghan currency introduced at the end of 2002.

Minister of information and culture, Sayed Raheen, higher education minister, Sherief Fayez, minister of environment and irrigation, Yusuf Nooristani, and Karzai's chief of staff and president of international relations, Said Tayeb Jawad, are the other Afghan-Americans in the cabinet and other senior positions. The minister of reconstruction, Amin Farang, is an Afghan from Germany

Anwar ul-Haq Ahadi, the governor of the Afghan Central Bank, was a professor of political science at Providence College in Rhode Island.

But the main powerbroker in 2002 was widely acknowledged to be President Bush's special representative to Afghanistan, Zalmay Khalilzad, another Afghan-American. He was largely seen to have been the one to persuade the former King

THE KING

King Zahir Shar returned to Kabul from Italy in April 2002 after 29 years in exile. For many Afghans, especially the older generation, the king's 40-year rule from 1933 is regarded as a period of peace and stability when women were educated and a free press encouraged. Zahir Shah was born on October 15 1914 and educated in Kabul and Paris. He became king in 1933 just hours after his father's assassination. But his cousin and a former prime minister, Mohammad Daud, deposed the king during a coup in July 1973 while he was receiving medical treatment in Italy, bringing to an end the rule of the Durrani dynasty and a monarchy in Afghanistan. Daud declared himself president of a new Republic of Afghanistan. In 2002 the king returned to Kabul from Rome expressing no political ambitions. Later that year he opened the June Loya Jirga grand assembly at which there were moves to have him reinstated, but behind-the-scenes negotiations won him title of 'Father of the Nation' and secured Hamid Karzai the position of president. King Zahir's wife, Queen Homaira, was buried in the royal family mausoleum in June 2002. She died in Italy at the age of 86 while waiting to rejoin her husband in Kabul. The queen is survived by seven of her nine children and by 14 grandchildren.

Zahir Shah to step down during the Loya Jirga in favour of Karzai. King Zahir accepted the title of 'Father of the Nation'.

Karzai tried to persuade a number of warlords during the Loya Jirga to take up government positions in Kabul, notably Herat governor Ismail Khan and Mazar strongman General Dostum. Dostum became deputy defence minister but spends much of his time in the north despite his sudden transformation, shirking military uniform for Western suits. There was little chance Ismail Khan would give up his strong base and money-earning capacity in the Herat region. Khan is rumoured to make US$280 million a year through lucrative customs revenue from undeclared over-the-border dealings with Iran.

ECONOMY

After 23 years of war, the country's infrastructure is shattered and the economy virtually non-existent. Today, Afghanistan depends heavily on foreign aid. In Tokyo in January 2002 the international community pledged four billion dollars over five years to the Central Asian state's reconstruction. However, that money is not coming into the country fast enough for many Afghans.

Historically, the mainstay of economic prosperity in Afghanistan has been agriculture. But the drought that has plagued Afghanistan for the past five years means the traditional crops are failing and the drought-resistant poppies are the new crop of choice for thousands of struggling farmers. It is fair to say that the only thriving form of income generation in Afghanistan today is the annual poppy harvest.

HAMID KARZAI

Hamid Karzai wasn't even at the December 2001 Bonn Peace Agreement when he was chosen as chairman of the Interim Administration. In the months that followed he was groomed for power and was elected president at the June 2002 Loya Jirga. He probably has one of the most difficult jobs in the world, chairing a cabinet of ministers who have fought each other for many years. He has been called the Mayor of Kabul as he struggles to assert his authority outside the capital city and bring the regional governors and warlords into line. On September 5, 2002, Karzai narrowly escaped death from assassination whilst under the protection of his US bodyguards in his hometown of Kandahar. The bodyguards killed the assassin and two others as Karzai's car sped away. The

Cultivation of this illicit crop stretches from Badakhstan in the far north to Helmand province in the south.

The opium economy has made Afghanistan the world's number-one producer of illicit opium. According to a United Nations Office on Drugs and Crime (UNODC) report in February 2003:

> Afghanistan's opium production increased fifteen fold since 1979, the year of
> the Soviet intervention. By the year 2000, the country was the source of

dramatic footage was filmed and seen worldwide on BBC TV. Karzai is a Pashtun and comes from the same clan as King Zahir Shah. In 1992 he was deputy foreign minister under President Rabbani. Karzai did support the Taliban for a brief period but they assassinated his father (a former parliamentarian) in 1999. Karzai continued the fight against the Taliban from Pakistan, often slipping over the border back into Afghanistan, even in October 2001 when he narrowly escaped capture. His brothers built up a successful chain of restaurants in the US, contributing funds to their brother's campaigning. Karzai married only in 1999. World leaders have feted Karzai since he took the reins of power in Afghanistan. His choice of flowing cloaks and Afghan hats, his charismatic style and fluency in English have won him many admirers.

70% of all illicit opium produced in the world. Following a decline in 2001, production resumed at high levels in 2002, again making Afghanistan the world's largest producer (followed by Myanmar and the Lao People's Democratic Republic), accounting for almost three quarters of global opium production.

The Taliban led a campaign against opium production, but very quickly after the collapse of their regime farmers went back to work. For poor farmers opium is a fast

Economy

way to earn more money; for regional warlords it is a source of great revenue. US State Department figures estimate that Afghanistan's opium crop in 2000 was 3,656 tonnes, or 72% of the world's total. This was an increase from only 31% in 1985.

In the cities, the growing economic sector is the NGO scene. The Foreign Ministry, which registers all the NGOs, logged more than 250 new NGOs by the end of 2002. Each NGO offers employment possibilities to tens of Afghans with positions ranging from engineering posts, project managers and domestic staff.

Traditional artefacts and handicrafts also help countless thousands of people to make a living. The carpet business is booming, though the inflated prices in central Kabul do not reflect in any way the income the carpet weavers earn in their far-flung rural villages.

Sadly the drought has decimated the flocks of the nomadic shepherds (or Kuchis). This traditional way of life and economic livelihood is under threat as the nomads give up their old ways of life and turn to the cities for their survival.

PEOPLE

The population of Afghanistan is estimated to be 27,755,775 (CIA World Factbook estimate, July 2002). In 2000, the United Nations Population Fund estimated the population of Afghanistan at some 22.7 million. The most recent census, though, was in 1979, when the population was reported to be about 15.5 million (UN website).

The population of Kabul can only be guessed at. A 1988 estimate puts it at 1,424,000; by 1994 the estimate was down to half that at 700,000. The figure now, with the fall of the Taliban and the return of refugee families from Pakistan and Iran, is estimated at between 1.5 and 2.5 million people.

That trend is reflected across Afghanistan. In all, it is estimated that some 2 million refugees returned to Afghanistan in 2002 and a further 1.5 million are expected in 2003. With the high number of returnees and the arrival of the international community, great strain is being placed on vital services such as sanitation, water and electricity.

There are four major ethnic groups in the country: Pashtuns (38–44%), Tajiks (25%), Hazaras (10–19%) and Uzbeks (6–8%). Other ethnic groups (12–13%) include Aimaks, Nuristanis, Baluchis, Turkmens and Kuchis.

The Taliban originated from the majority Pashtun south, and the Northern Alliance, now in control in Kabul, comes from the Tajik north. President Karzai is a Pashtun and is having to balance the different ethnic groups in his cabinet.

LANGUAGE

The official languages are Pashto (35%) and Afghan Persian or Dari (50%). Other languages include Turkic, Uzbek and Turkmen (11%) and some 30 minor languages, mainly Baluchi and Pashai (4%). Most Afghans will be bilingual in Pashto and Dari. In Kabul, Dari is more widely spoken now with the change of regime from the Pashto-speaking Taliban to the Dari-speaking Northern Alliance.

Afghanistan clearly betrays its role as an important crossroads for the Indo-European language heritage. Regardless of where you are from, many words will seem

Language

familiar. A few examples include *bas*, which in Dari means 'that's enough!' The word has more than a passing resemblance to *basta*, the word for 'that's enough' in Italian and Spanish. Similarly, the word in Dari for a room is *camera*, the same as the Italian.

As a visitor in Kabul it's very much appreciated if you have key words in Dari and Pashto on the tip of your tongue (see *Language* appendix, page 154). You will find English is widely spoken, especially in Kabul itself and among those who were refugees in Pakistan. Russian, German and French are also popular foreign languages, as well as Iranian (Persian Farsi) and Pakistani Urdu.

RELIGION

About 99% of Afghans belong to the Islamic faith (Sunni Muslim 84%, Shi'a Muslim 15%) with small groups of Sikhs, Hindus, Christians and Jews.

Religion is a major part of daily life and men will pray five times a day and go to the city mosques on Fridays. You'll hear the call to prayer across the city.

Religious holidays are also important and the city becomes very quiet on these days as people stay at home or travel to see their families.

EDUCATION

The education system in Afghanistan has been wrecked after 23 years of war. During the Taliban regime from 1996 to 2001 women and girls were denied any form of education. In March 2002 some three million children went back to school at the start of a new school year, the first time they had been able to for years.

Thousands of girls were eagerly running to school with their rucksacks every day.

The government, with the support of international agencies, organised a huge back-to-school campaign. Millions are being spent on the retraining of teachers, the reconstruction of schools and the printing of textbooks.

In Kabul a number of schools and the university have seen substantial repairs and support. Many departments at the university have received a lot of support and libraries are being restocked and computers installed. Teachers and lecturers have attended courses abroad.

Kabul University, founded in 1932 in the much destroyed west of the city, is once again a thriving campus but extremely run-down. Riots in November 2002 led to at least two deaths and serious injuries for more than ten people as hundreds of students protested about poor living conditions and a lack of electricity. Kabul University used to be one of Asia's great educational institutions. It was built with American money and Western academics used to lecture in the faculties.

CULTURE

Afghanistan sits on a historical crossroads where many cultures have met and mingled – Persian, Greek, Buddhist, Hindu and Islamic – and the country has many cultural and natural treasures. Unfortunately not many of them have withstood the passage of time.

When you mention historical sites in Afghanistan, most people will cite the Taliban's wanton destruction of the magnificent statues of Buddha in the central highland city of Bamyian in the Hazarajat in March 2001.

Culture

Certainly, the Taliban period has been one of the most destructive for the country's cultural heritage. Their influence can be put on a par with the havoc wreaked by the Mongol hordes who flattened Balkh, Herat, Ghazni and Bamyian under Genghis Khan in the 13th century. Though they didn't flatten cities, the Taliban systematically set about looting and ransacking the country's artistic treasure trove. Throughout their regime historical artefacts were smuggled out to Pakistan and into the West. On February 26 2001 Mullah Omar decreed 'all non-Islamic statues and tombs' to be destroyed. Only a month later, the 2,000 year old Buddha statues were rased to the ground by tank fire and explosives.

Today, the looting goes on. Archaeological sites are being illegally excavated and plundered with no care. Reports suggest this ongoing business could now be more lucrative than the revived opium trade. All the major museums in the country have been emptied and significant archaeological sites at Jam, Lashkar Gah, Tepe Sardar, Balkh, Ai Khanum, Kapsa and Hadda are under daily threat.

In June 2002 the 65m-tall Minaret of Jam, built in 1194 in west-central Afghanistan, was added to UNESCO's World Heritage list. It is the world's second tallest minaret and the site is the first in Afghanistan to be on the UNESCO list. But it has also been added to the List of World Heritage in Danger, and illegal excavations continue near the site. Sadly, artefacts are being dug up in broad daylight and loaded onto donkeys for transportation to Herat where they are sold on to dealers.

In the capital, Kabul, the museum was considered to be the biggest treasure-

MUSIC

After long years of suppression under the prohibitive Taliban regime, when even music was banned as un-Islamic, Afghan's rich musical tradition is making a comeback. In summer months it is not uncommon to find musicians playing live Afghan music at garden parties. The traditional Afghan troubadours are also popular again at weddings. This said, in 2002 there were several reports of musicians in Kabul being shot dead at wedding parties by religious hardliners who object to the practice.

Look out for recordings of Afghanistan's most famous singer-songwriter of modern time, Ahmad Zahir. A legend in his own lifetime, he was the charismatic playboy son of one of Afghanistan's most influential parliamentarians. According to accounts from the time, Ahmad Zahir was also very handsome and a big hit with the ladies. He met his end after a torrid affair with a married woman. Her husband shot Zahir in revenge, thus ending the career of one of the country's best-loved entertainers and a leading proponent of Afghan musical culture.

trove the city boasted. Today, this repository of ancient Buddhist and Indo-Greek art has lost much of its extensive collection. Two thirds of the 100,000 items in Kabul Museum disappeared, adding to the loss suffered during the 1991–96 looting.

Culture

A programme to return items sold or taken abroad illegally is to be started as soon as the museum has been made sufficiently secure. However this will be a difficult, indeed, virtually impossible task. Finding the missing artefacts will take tremendous detective work. A great wealth of historical pieces have been lost and destroyed forever.

The Ministry of Information and Culture and UNESCO are leading efforts to reopen the museum and have launched a worldwide appeal for artefacts to be returned. Early in 2002 the banner, in English, on the museum wall read: 'A Nation Can Stay Alive When Its Culture Stays Alive'.

Bradt Travel Guides is a partner to the new 'know before you go' campaign, recently launched by the UK Foreign and Commonwealth Office. By combining the up-to-date advice of the FCO with the in-depth knowledge of Bradt authors, you'll ensure that your trip will be as trouble-free as possible.

www.fco.gov.uk/knowbeforeyougo

Background

WHEN TO VISIT

Kabul has one of the most beautiful natural locations of any city in the world. Whenever you choose to visit you are in for a treat. Nestled in the Kabul River Valley almost 1,800m (5,900ft) above sea level, it has an enviable climate and four distinct and equally charming seasons. Perhaps the best time to visit is in April or May when the temperatures are mild, the air clear and the sky a cloudless, cobalt blue. But every season has its attractions. In winter the breathtaking mountains surrounding the city are covered in snow. During these winter months Kabul is cold and wet with some snowfall and bitterly cold night temperatures (−10°C to −18°C). The end of winter sees the city transformed into something of a mud-bath as the snow melts and most of the 88mm of annual precipitation falls. By April, however, the days are warm during daylight hours. As the spring develops, the famous Kabul climate comes into its own with temperatures hovering around a delightful 28°C. In the summer months those temperatures climb into the 30s, and the city becomes dust prone. (However, compared to the lowland cities like Jalalabad and Kandahar where temperatures reach 50°C, Kabul is considered a haven.) By September the heat is again receding and the nights beginning to draw in. But it is not until November that the daytime temperatures become chilly again.

Take the numerous holidays and religious festivals (remembering dates vary depending on the moon) into account if your visit is short and connected with urgent business. Official holidays are sometimes declared just days in advance and official visits from visiting presidents or a senior foreign visitor often means the airport will be closed suddenly and streets in the city blocked. Security alerts will also close down major sections of the city with regular checkpoints.

For business try and avoid Ramadan (October in 2003), Eid (February in 2003) and the first week of the Naw Rouz celebrations (March) as working hours are minimal at these times and official staff very rarely to be found. Afghan embassies abroad will also close for holidays (sometimes for the whole week for Eid).

PUBLIC HOLIDAYS AND IMPORTANT DATES

Naw-Rouz (Solar New Year)	March 21
Celebration of the Islamic Revolution in Afghanistan	April 28
National Labour Day	May 1
Remembrance Day for Martyrs and Disabled	May 4
Independence Day (from Britain in 1919)	August 19
Ahmad Shah Massoud Day	September 9

Religious dates 2003 (may vary according to the sighting of the moon)

Arafa	February 10
Ashora Day	March 13
Eid ul-Athha (Feast of the Sacrifice)	February 11–13
Eid-ul-Milad-ul-Nabi (Birth of the Prophet Mohammad)	May 14
First Day of Ramadan	October 26
Eid-ul-Ramadan	November 25–27

To calculate the Islamic year, subtract 621 years from the Western Gregorian calendar date. For example: 2003 – 621 = 1382.

PREPARING YOUR VISIT

We've listed a number of websites in *Appendix 4* where you can brief yourself on the current situation, latest developments and background. It is also worth getting *Afghanistan – Essential Field Guides to Humanitarian and Conflict Zones* by Edward Girardet and Jonathan Walker. Originally published in 1998, a revised edition is due out in 2003.

If you're part of a UK NGO you'll be able to subscribe to regular emails from BAAG (British Agencies Afghanistan Group). The BAAG website (www.baag.org.uk) is also regularly updated.

You might like to subscribe to a daily email digest of news copied from various world publications by some Afghans in Australia, email: info@mobycapital.com.

IAM, International Assistance Mission, a non-profit charitable organisation with 35 years' experience of working in Afghanistan, runs orientation courses every other month at US$150 per person covering topics such as beliefs and practices of Islam, culture, history and security. IAM is based at Sarak-e-Shora, Karte 3; tel: 020 250 1185, +88 216 5420 1012; email: staffdevelop@iamafg.org.

ACBAR, the Agency Coordinating Body for Afghan Relief, House 12, Jami Wat, Shahre Naw, tel: 070 28 2090, 020 229 9208, web: www.acbar.org, continuously updates its information on NGOs working in Kabul into a very comprehensive list.

TOURIST INFORMATION

There's an **Afghan Tourist Organisation** information office at Kabul airport (tel: 070 27 6378; open 08.30–15.00) but with little information. It tends to operate as a place to arrange an officially accredited translator or car. The ATO also has offices at the Intercontinental Hotel in Kabul, in Herat and Bamyian and is planning to open offices in Mazar, Kandahar and elsewhere.

Good **maps** of Afghanistan and Central Asia are available from Stanfords (12–14 Long Acre, London WC2E 9LP; tel: 020 7836 1321; web: www.stanfords.co.uk) and from AIMS (Afghanistan Information Management Service; web: www.aims.org.pk).

In Kabul, maps and other guides and historical books are available, as well as copies of the indispensable 1970s' books by Afghanistan expert Nancy Hatch Dupree: *An Historical Guide to Afghanistan* and *An Historical Guide to Kabul*. Most of the street bookshops and the Intercontinental Hotel bookshop have copies of these (for US$5–10) and other titles.

Updates for this guide will be placed online at www.kabulguide.net.

TOUR OPERATORS

In 2002 two UK tour operators organised trips to Afghanistan and they have plans for further tours. Destinations include Kabul, Bamyian, Herat, and Mazar-i-Sharif. There are concerns about travelling by road, though internal flights with Ariana are unreliable and UN flights are expensive.

Practicalities

Hinterland Travel Geoff Hann, 12 The Enterdent, Godstone, Surrey RH9 8EG; tel: 01883 743584; fax: 743584; email: hinterland@tinyworld.co.uk
LIVE Travel Phil Haines, 120 Hounslow Rd, Twickenham TW2 7HB; tel: 020 8894 6104; fax: 0870 138 6931; email: phil.haines@live-travel.com; web: www.live-travel.com

TIME DIFFERENCE

GMT + four hours and 30 minutes is the time difference (ie: 12.00 GMT = 16.30 in Afghanistan). The clock never goes back or forward during the year in Afghanistan.

Watch out if you're travelling through or dealing with Pakistan. Pakistan is GMT + five hours, but changes its clocks on different days from most of the rest of the world. So when you're in Afghanistan you may be 30 minutes or one hour 30 minutes behind Pakistan depending on the clock changes.

To catch VOA or BBC World Service top-of-the-hour news programmes, tune in on the half-hour. Dubai is GMT + four hours.

VISAS

There is a lot of red tape associated with working in and travelling to Afghanistan. The visa procedure is of course no exception.

In early 2002 most people arrived in Afghanistan without a visa as the embassies abroad were not working properly (some were still issuing visas with Taliban regime stamps). Even up to August 2002 some people were arriving without visas and able to enter the country. It is not advisable to try entering without a visa now.

In London a six-month multiple-entry visa in February 2003 cost £60. You'll need to fill in the application form, attach a passport photo and submit a passport valid for a minimum of three to six months, and a letter of introduction. The Pakistan High Commission (35 Lowndes Square, London SW1X 9JN; tel: 020 7664 9200; email: informationdivision@highcommission-uk.gov.pk; web: www.pakmission-uk.gov.pk) processed a six-month, double-entry, five-day transit visa for Pakistan for £60 in February 2003. Fill in the form and submit two passport photos and a letter of introduction. Submit visas before 12.30 and they'll be ready at 16.30.

In Rome a three-month multiple-entry visa for Afghanistan costs €100.

In Washington visa prices vary depending on how quickly you want it processed (US$50 within two weeks, US$70 within three days and US$100 on the same day).

Once in country it is possible to get extensions and new visas from the passport office in Kabul (on Passport Lane, just off the Interior Ministry Road) with the relevant documents such as a letter from an NGO. In Kabul a six-month, multiple-entry visa for Pakistan costs US$120.

Afghanistan embassies and missions

UK Embassy of Afghanistan, 31 Prince's Square, London SW7 1QU; tel: +44 20 7589 8891; fax: 7581 3452; email: pa.afghanembassy@btinternet.com. Open 09.30–13.30, Monday to Friday. Visas can be done within one hour 30 minutes.

USA Embassy of Afghanistan, 2341 Wyoming Av, Washington DC 20008; tel: +1 202 483 6410; fax: 483 6488; email: info@embassyofafghanistan.org; web: www.embassyofafghanistan.org.

Australia Embassy of Afghanistan, PO Box 155. Deakin West, Canberra, ACT 2600; tel: +61 (2) 6282 7311; fax: +61 (2) 6282 7322; email: admin@afghanembassy.net; web: www.afghanembassy.net

There are also Afghan missions in Austria, Bangladesh, Bulgaria, China, Czech Republic, Egypt, France, Germany (Bonn and Berlin), India, Indonesia, Iran, Iraq, Italy, Kazakhstan, Kuwait, Kyrgyzstan, Malaysia, Pakistan (Islamabad, Karachi, Quetta, Peshawar), Poland, Russia, Saudi Arabia, Sudan, Switzerland, Syria, Tajikistan, Turkey, Turkmenistan, Ukraine, United Arab Emirates and Uzbekistan.

GETTING THERE AND AWAY

On arrival (and departure) at Kabul airport fill in an embarkation (disembarkation) form and you'll get your passport stamped with an entry (exit) visa. On arrival present your passport with the page open at the Afghan visa.

Travel agencies and tour operators in Kabul

The **Kapisa Travel Agency** (tel: 070 28 3498, 070 27 8187) on Shahre Naw Road, just down from the Emergency Hospital and close to the Cinema Park, sells flights to Tehran with Mahan Air, to Baku with Azerbaijan Airlines and to Ankara.

There's also a branch of the London-based **Afghan Travel Centre** (107 Great Portland Street, London W1W 6QG; tel: 020 7580 7020; fax: 020 7580 7101; email: abdul@travelhorizons.co.uk) at the Karwansara Guesthouse.

At **Asia International Transit Transport** (tel: 070 27 7629) in Wazir Akbar Khan, Street 14, House 4, you can get foreign magazines and newspapers. They can organise a private car for US$100 to take you the Torkham route to Peshawar in Pakistan, and they also run cars from Kandahar to Quetta in Pakistan. They can also organise a US$5 ticket in a bus with air conditioning, which takes nine hours to get to Peshawar.

Flying to Kabul

Most people visiting or coming to work in Kabul will probably arrive by air in one of three ways: on board a United Nations plane operated by UNHAS (United Nations Humanitarian Air Services); with Ariana Afghan Airlines from Dubai or Islamabad; or with Pakistan International Airlines (PIA) from Islamabad. There are also flights from Baku, Dushanbe and Tehran.

Ariana and PIA are usually referred to as 'Inshallah Airways' or 'Please Inform Allah' for PIA. Though it is also worth remembering that in Bosnia during the conflict UN flights were known as Maybe Airways (and you received a stamp in your passport to that effect).

Foreign military staff are likely to arrive by air at Kabul airport or at the main international military base at Bagram airport about 45 minutes' drive outside Kabul.

UNHAS

UNHAS flights are still the favoured way for most people flying from Dubai and Islamabad and within Afghanistan, but they're not the cheapest.

UNHAS operates flights to Dubai and Islamabad using a Fokker F-28 64-seater plane chartered from Air Quarius in Johannesburg (web: www.airquarius.co.za). Schedules change monthly so always check, but generally there are two flights a week from Dubai on Wednesdays and Sundays and two out of Kabul on Saturdays and Tuesdays. The rest of the week there are flights from Islamabad.

UNHAS Dubai flights cost US$400 one way for everyone but are restricted to staff from UN agencies, internationally approved NGOs and diplomats.

For NGOs, domestic flights on Beachcraft planes to Mazar-i-Sharif, Herat, Kandahar and Chaghcharan cost US$100. The shorter hops to Bamyian and Jalalabad cost US$50. Flights to Islamabad cost US$100.

If you're not on the approved list a one way from Islamabad will cost you US$600, Herat US$600, Kandahar US$440 and Mazar US$290.

There's a 'first-come, first-served' basis and there's no guarantee on flights taking off or seats being granted. In the winter bad weather and snow can seriously disrupt schedules, leaving passengers stranded in Dubai or Islamabad for days whilst the backlog is cleared.

Luggage allowance has gone up from 20kg to 40kg (including hand luggage) and excess luggage is charged at US$2 a kilo. Pre-booked excess luggage can be arranged with the cargo department.

Bookings can be made in person or by email and tickets need to be picked up in advance. Check-in is at Terminal 2 in Dubai and at Kabul and Islamabad airports, two hours in advance for international flights and one hour in advance for internal flights.

Getting there and away

FLYING INTO AFGHANISTAN
Khorshied Nusratty

My heart started to beat stronger and faster as the plane began to descend into the dusty, stark beauty of this country. Here and there, a few green and lush valleys appeared, dotted with villages the same colour as the pale mountains. As far as the eye could see, there were jagged peaks and vast plains that made up this land, and the drought was evident even from my vista in the sky. I was returning to Afghanistan this time to live, to work, and to find myself in a country that was struggling to find itself.

Afghanistan is made up of city-states, provinces, ethnic groups and tribal distinctions that keep it strong in its diversity but also keep it apart. You could see the distinctions everywhere, from the various languages and dialects spoken to the prejudice and competition that existed between the Pashtuns, Tajiks and Hazara peoples. On so many levels, the Afghan people were stubbornly proud of who they were and how they wouldn't allow any foreign influence guide or destroy them. They had proven that throughout 23 years of war fighting against Soviets, Mujaheddin factions, and the Taliban. But in this process they had also succeeded in destroying themselves and their country, tearing apart any cohesive fabric that had held them together as a country and a people. Now they were searching to regain some semblance of truth, some identity of who they were and what they would become as an Afghan people.

I found myself drawn to Afghanistan like a moth to a flame. The clarity of vision and hope that I felt coming here was somewhat startling to me; I felt so sure, so inspired about what I could do and how I could contribute to rebuild this country, although as an Afghan-American woman I wasn't that clear of my role quite yet. I was straddling two worlds: one foot firmly planted in the new world of the United States where I was born and raised; the other stepping into a nearly forgotten world, where I could trace and discover the origins of my father's culture and my lineage. This world was filled with undeniable riches and mysteries, pain and pleasure, a landscape of extremes where life appeared very real and genuine. I could never turn away from the shining eyes of a beautiful child whose smile charmed me in an instant and melted my heart. What did it matter if by giving them a small handful of Afghanis I might be contributing to their thinking that begging was a way out of their extreme poverty? Perhaps by the mere fact that I had come to live in Afghanistan at this hugely insecure yet historic time might show them that there was hope, that choices existed, that they had to believe in themselves at all costs. And never give up.

Khorshied Nusratty came to Afghanistan in June 2002. She is the founder of Artists for Afghanistan Foundation, an NGO established to help preserve the arts and culture of Afghanistan through creative projects (see page 172).

UNHAS **in Kabul** is based inside the World Food Programme compound just beyond the Char-i-Zanbaq roundabout and across from UNAMA compound B. Tel: 070 28 2817–826, extension 2443 for flight information, arrival and departure times; extension 2444/45/46 for seat availability; email: kabul.unhas@wfp.org. UNHAS is open every day, 08.00–12.00 and 12.30–16.00, except Fridays.

In Pakistan UNHAS is based at House 4, Street 5, F/8-3; tel: +92 51 2264101, 226 4077, 226 4203, 226 4284; fax: +92 51 226 4054; email: islamabad.unhas@wfp.org. You can also contact Ajmal Amini (tel: +92 320 450 7255; email: ajmal.amini@wfp.org) or Howard Meredith (tel: +92 320 450 7256; email: howard.meredith@wfp.org).

There are also UNAMA flights both within the country and to Dubai that are restricted to UNAMA staff and those with special clearance.

Ariana Afghan Airlines
(web: www.flyariana.com)

You'll see most of the old Ariana planes destroyed on the outskirts of Kabul airport but the airline is slowly expanding both its fleet and schedule.

Ariana destinations include Frankfurt, Moscow, Istanbul, Dubai, Sharjah, Tehran, Amritsar, Delhi and Islamabad. Ariana also flies to Herat, sometimes making a stop in Mazar. Flights from Dubai are on Wednesdays and Sundays. Prices vary but in March 2003 returns from Kabul to Delhi cost around US$420; Dubai US$341; Tehran US$310; Islamabad US$200; one way to Istanbul US$365; one way to Frankfurt US$495.

There are concerns about the airworthiness of the Ariana fleet and the maintenance that is carried out on the three Airbuses and three Boeing 727s that are used for international flights. UN staff can use Ariana for private trips but they waive all their UN insurance. Many journalists and aid workers now use Ariana from Dubai as it avoids the extra day that's necessary when travelling through Islamabad. However, Ariana passengers often report that the Dubai to Kabul flight is frequently up to six hours late in departing from Dubai. One traveller said she'd woken up in Tehran unexpectedly on the Frankfurt to Kabul via Istanbul flight.

In Kabul Ariana Airlines are to be found in Wazir Akbar Khan, Street 13, near the Embassy of Pakistan, tel: 020 210 0271, 210 0269. There's an Ariana Information desk at Kabul airport, tel: 020 230 1344. There is also an office at the Intercontinental Hotel (tel: 020 220 1516, 210 0271) for the latest details as the schedules change frequently. The Ariana website has up-to-date details and a list of offices and Afghan embassies abroad.

A number of travel agents can book Ariana tickets. Check the Ariana website for a list. The prices may vary but in Dubai a one-way ticket to Kabul from Dubai costs US$185; a return costs US$370. It is worth booking in advance through a travel agent (so you get your name on the list) though tickets can be bought at the airport providing there is space on the plane.

Eisa Travels **in Dubai** can arrange tickets for collection at Dubai Terminal 2; tel: +971 4 295 5444; fax: +971 4 295 5554; email: eisafgsc@emirates.net.ae.

In London Abdul Karim at the Afghan Travel Centre (107 Great Portland Street,

Getting there and away

Practicalities

TRAVELLING ON ARIANA
Some thoughts on Ariana from a UN traveller in November 2002:

Ariana was quite an experience. Three hours' delay in Dubai (as we were waiting we realised that there was a UNHAS flight flying the same morning – UNHAS had just changed their schedule – ARGH!). Anyway, we were up for adventure with a big A, and Ariana is obviously the right choice. Actually, the flight was very pleasant – an Airbus offered by Air India (quite colourful seats), Afghan crew and Russian pilot. Security demonstrations were succinct, no mention of lifejackets. Anyway who needs lifejackets once over land-locked Afghanistan? The views from the plane were superb now that there is snow covering most of the mountains. Smooth (yes!) landing at Kabul airport; with remixed Abba as background music, and then uncontrolled distribution of luggage that took approximately one hour 30 minutes. In conclusion, if you want a multi-cultural experience go for Ariana. If you have a strict schedule don't.

London W1W 6QG; tel: +44 (0)20 7580 7020; fax: +44 (0)20 7580 7101; email: abdul@travelhorizons.co.uk) can organise flights to Kabul (Dubai to Kabul one way is £299, a return costs £499) and visas.

In **Germany** (Düsseldorf) Ehsan Shorish can organise your Frankfurt-to-Kabul trip and arrange for a Dubai-to-Kabul ticket to be collected in Dubai. Tel: +49 (0)211 168 8870; fax: +49 (0)211 168 88777; email: reisebuero-ctm@t-online.de.

Other airlines

Air Serv PACTEC office in Wazir Akbar Khan, Street 12; tel: +93 70 28 2679; email: bookingkbl@pactec.net. Islamabad tel: +92 51 210 5261, 300 850 8816; email: pakbooking@airserv.org; web: www.airserv.org. Air Serv is a humanitarian charter-flight service operating across Afghanistan and to Pakistan.

Azerbaijan Airlines Charahe Ansane; tel: 070 28 4207; Baku tel: +994 12 93 4004, 93 7121; web: www.icd-azal.com. Three flights a week from Baku to Kabul are operated on Sundays, Wednesdays and Thursdays (approximately US$340 return). There are several possibilities for international connections (eg: US$650 return to Paris). Visas can be obtained on arrival in Baku for US$40.

Emirates (web: www.emirates.com) Emirates regularly fly to Islamabad from Dubai with excellent international connections through Dubai.

ICRC Shahre Naw between Qali Fatullah main road and Shar-e-Shahid road; tel: 070 27 9078, 020 220 0326. The International Committee of the Red Cross operates internal flights and flights to Peshawar, Pakistan, which NGO members can book.

Mahan Office at Kabul airport; tel: 020 230 1337, 070 22 4442; web: www.mahanairlines.com. Mahan Airlines flies from Tehran once a week to Kabul. Mahan Airlines can also arrange Tehran transit visas from their office at the airport (open

Getting there and away

08.30–16.30). Round trip Kabul to Tehran costs approximately US$300.

Pakistan International Airlines (web: www.piac.com.pk) PIA flies from Islamabad to and from Kabul once a week every Thursday afternoon (US$200 one way). PIA also operates an extensive worldwide schedule with flights direct from Islamabad to London, Manchester and Birmingham. Other PIA destinations include New York, Toronto, Frankfurt, Paris, Rome, Athens, Amsterdam and further east including Tokyo, Bangkok, Kuala Lumpur and Jakarta.

Tajik Air Regional office in Germany (Munich): tel: +49 89 975 94 210; fax: +49 89 975 94 216; email: gartjk@i-dail.de; web: www.tajnet.com/~tajikair. Operates a flight from Dushanbe to Kabul, usually on Sundays, though the plane has been spotted at Kabul airport on a Wednesday.

Travel by road: the Khyber Pass

Perhaps one of the most romantic ways to travel in to Afghanistan is overland through the evocative Khyber Pass. Although the current political climate means the pass can be a perilous undertaking, it remains a breathtaking journey.

It should be emphasised the 53km passage through the Hindu Kush mountain range is probably the least dangerous part of the journey. On either side of the Khyber Pass is what is known colloquially as Pashtunistan, home to the fiery Pashtuns, the ethnic group known for its proud, uncompromising beliefs and traditions. On the Pakistan side of the border this means the Federally Administered Tribal Areas which, though nominally under Pakistan Central Government control, are in reality ungovernable from any legislative standpoint.

This region is notorious for being the lawless area where many Al Qaeda fighters found refuge after fleeing US air strikes in the Tora Bora region of Afghanistan in December 2001.

On the Afghan side the pass is still controlled by tribal chiefs who make their living by smuggling drugs. Much of the region is currently in a state of extreme instability owing to the clampdown on poppy production, the crop that produces opium and heroin. The poppy eradication scheme has led many farmers to riot as their livelihoods go up in smoke. The volatile situation is compounded by reports of night-time letter droppings urging the local population to kill foreigners.

Despite this, or perhaps because of it, the Khyber Pass remains one of the most famous passes in the world and the best land route between Pakistan and Afghanistan. Quite aside from the latest developments, the Khyber Pass has had a long and bloody history. Conquering armies used it to annex fresh territories. It was also part of the famous Silk Route that has been used by traders and merchants for centuries. To travel along this historic road is to live a part of that legend first hand.

Pakistan controls the Khyber Pass and if you are travelling in from Pakistan you will need a permit. Foreigners are not allowed in the Tribal Areas without a No-Objection Certificate for security reasons. This has to be requested from the Khyber Tribal Agency in Peshawar at least 24 hours before departure. The agency is a department of the government of the North West Frontier Province and is housed in an old colonial building near University Town in Peshawar. Currently the permit costs 120 Pakistani Rupees per person.

You will also be compelled to take an armed Pakistani guard with you when you travel. The guard is provided by the Khyber Agency and is for your protection for the stretch of the journey through the Tribal Area up to the border crossing with Afghanistan.

Oddly enough, you don't need to make arrangements with the Khyber Tribal Agency if you are travelling in to Pakistan from Afghanistan, though it would be wise for you to request permission nonetheless if you can. (You would need to exploit any contacts you might have in Peshawar to do this.)

After heading out past the so-called Smuggler's Bazaar on the northwest outskirts of Peshawar, the road quickly leads through the Sulaiman Hills which form the western barrier of Pakistan. The hills dip down in places, leaving a passage sometimes as broad as 1.5km and sometimes as narrow as 16m. The pass itself begins near Jamrud Fort 18km from Peshawar and extends about 20km beyond the border into Afghanistan. At the Torkham border crossing, the Pakistan Tourism Development Corporation has a motel-cum-information centre which is closed at present due to unsettled conditions in Afghanistan.

It takes roughly two hours to get from Peshawar to the Torkham border crossing, but the road is usually heavily congested with lorries carrying contraband across the porous border. Don't forget to look out for the imposing home of the world-famous drugs baron and Pakistan's most famous smuggler Ayub Afridi. If you are travelling with someone who has some local knowledge they will have no trouble in pointing out the huge fortress-home. If not, it is on the Pakistan side of the border about 40 minutes out from Peshawar on your left. Really, you can't miss it! Afridi is reputed to be on the CIA's wanted list and legend has it that the former Pakistani parliamentarian is so rich he offered to pay off Pakistan's foreign debt if charges against him were waived. The Pakistan government refused this offer, but Afridi remains a powerful influence in the region and one of the wealthiest men in Pakistan.

Also keep an eye out for Jamrud Fort that lies amongst low hills, capped with pickets manned by the Khyber Rifles who are one of the oldest military units of the North West Frontier Province (NWFP). The Khyber Rifles, originally known as Khyber Jezailchis, were set up in 1878 as a semi-official armed outfit. Each man carried his own rifle (Jezail). The purpose of the unit was to prevent the various tribes making incursions along the line of control between Afghanistan and Pakistan.

Heading down in to Torkham you will find a veritable bedlam of people, vehicles, border guards, hawkers and porters. You need to get an exit stamp for your passport on your way out of both Pakistan and Afghanistan. These are available from the ramshackle buildings that house the passport control officials either side of no-man's land. The queues are long and in the winter those waiting for the exit stamp literally freeze. Torkham is one of the highest points of the Khyber Pass.

Foreigners are allowed to queue jump, but this can cause an already fractious queue to turn to open revolt. Always be courteous and sensitive towards those you are bypassing if your find yourself being whisked past by officials.

Getting there and away

Everything is handwritten into vast logbooks. Be prepared to give your name, profession, place and date of issue of passport, nationality and date of birth. The process is laborious.

Customs officials are usually nowhere to be seen and probably haven't been seen at Torkham for decades if the amount of contraband going through is anything to go by.

From the exit point of the country you are leaving you will need to head through no-man's land to immigration of the country you are entering. This seems to be somewhat quicker than the exit procedure. Again everything is logged by hand into massive ledgers. Be sure you get the correct passport stamps: one exit and one entry. By mishap one of our party ended up with two entry stamps and had to go back for a correction.

From here the journey to Jalalabad takes about two to two-and-a-half hours passing through the stark magnificence of the Sarobi Pass. Here the geographical drama of the jagged mountain peaks highlights the engineering brilliance of the road-builders who first carved out the way.

From Jalalabad it is another three hours to Kabul. For safety purposes, it is advised you make as few stops as possible and ensure you get to your destination before dusk.

Clearly this journey cannot be made without valid visas for both Afghanistan and Pakistan.

HEALTH

with Dr Felicity Nicholson

Life expectancy in Afghanistan is just 46 years for Afghan men and 45 years for women. The UN reports that six million people don't have access to basic health services, only 13% of people have access to safe drinking water and a mere 12% have access to adequate sanitation facilities. It stands to reason, then, that you should go well prepared.

Preparations

Be sure to have a full health check-up before travelling; no-one should consider travel to Afghanistan if they have any serious health conditions. Ensure, too, that you have all essential dental work carried out before you arrive.

Vaccinations

The only absolute requirement for Afghanistan is a **yellow fever** certificate if you are travelling from an infected area (some sub-Saharan and South American countries) or if you hold a passport from these countries. It would be wise, therefore, to check before you go. If required, a yellow fever vaccination needs to be taken at least ten days before travel. Other vaccinations are not mandatory but are recommended. For shorter trips it is wise to be up to date with **tetanus**, **diphtheria** and **polio** (all ten-yearly). A single dose of **hepatitis A** vaccine (Havrix Monodose or Avaxim) will provide cover for a year and can be backed up with a booster dose to give at least

LONG-HAUL FLIGHTS
Felicity Nicholson

There is growing evidence, albeit circumstantial, that long-haul air travel increases the risk of developing deep vein thrombosis. This condition is potentially life threatening, but it should be stressed that the danger to the average traveller is slight.

Certain risk factors specific to air travel have been identified. These include immobility, compression of the veins at the back of the knee by the edge of the seat, the decreased air pressure and slightly reduced oxygen in the cabin, and dehydration. Consuming alcohol may exacerbate the situation by increasing fluid loss and encouraging immobility. In theory everyone is at risk, but those at highest risk are:

- Passengers on journeys of longer than eight hours duration
- People over 40
- People with heart disease, cancer or clotting disorders
- People who have had recent surgery, especially on the legs
- Women on the pill or other oestrogen therapy
- Pregnancy
- People who are very tall (over 6ft/1.8m) or short (under 5ft/1.5m)

Practicalities

A deep vein thrombosis (DVT) is a clot of blood that forms in the leg veins. Symptoms include swelling and pain in the calf or thigh. The skin may feel hot to touch and becomes discoloured (light blue-red). A DVT is not dangerous in itself, but if a clot breaks down then it may travel to the lungs (pulmonary embolus). Symptoms of a pulmonary embolus (PE) include chest pain, shortness of breath and coughing up small amounts of blood.

Symptoms of a DVT rarely occur during the flight, and typically occur within three days of arrival, although symptoms of a DVT or PE have been reported up to two weeks later.

Anyone who suspects that they have these symptoms should see a doctor immediately as anticoagulation (blood thinning) treatment can be given.

Prevention of DVT
To reduce the risk of thrombosis, remember:

- Whilst waiting to board the plane, try to walk around rather than sit.
- During the flight drink plenty of water (at least two small glasses every hour).
- Avoid excessive tea, coffee and alcohol.
- Perform leg-stretching exercises, such as pointing the toes up and down.
- Move around the cabin when practicable.

Health

ten years' cover. Although it may cost around £100 for both doses, it is well worth taking as hepatitis A can cause debilitating disease. The newer **typhoid** vaccines (eg: Typhim Vi) are more effective than the older ones, have fewer side effects and are worth taking except at short notice for trips or a week or less.

For longer trips of four weeks or more, **rabies** and **hepatitis B** vaccine should be considered. These vaccines ideally consist of three doses and the course should be started between three and four weeks before you travel. It is wise therefore to plan your trip well in advance and to go your doctor or a travel clinic at least six weeks before departure.

Travel clinics and health information

A full list of current travel clinic websites worldwide is available on www.istm.org/. For other journey preparation information, consult ftp://ftp.shoreland.com/pub/shorecg.rtf or www.tripprep.com. The following are some of the major clinics worldwide:

UK

British Airways Travel Clinic and Immunisation Service 3 clinics in London: 156 Regent St, W1B 5LB (no appointments); 101 Cheapside, EC1V6DT (tel: 020 7606 2977); 115 Buckingham Palace Rd, SW1W 9SJ (Victoria Station; tel: 020 7233 6661); see also www.britishairways.com/travelclinics.

Trailfinders Immunisation Centre 194 Kensington High St, London W8 7RG; tel: 020 7938 3999

Irish Republic
Tropical Medical Bureau Grafton Street Medical Centre, Grafton Buildings, 34 Grafton St, Dublin 2; tel: 1 671 9200; web: www.tmb.ie

USA
Center for Disease Control 1600 Clifton Rd, Atlanta, GA 30333; tel: 877 FYI TRIP; 800 311 3435; web: www.cdc.gov/travel. The central source of travel information in the USA. Each summer they publish the invaluable Health Information for International Travel, available from the Division of Quarantine at the above address.

Canada
IAMAT (International Association for Medical Assistance to Travellers) Suite 1, 1287 St Clair Av W, Toronto, Ontario M6E 1B8; tel: 416 652 0137; web: www.sentex.net/~iamat

Australia, New Zealand, Thailand
TMVC Tel: 1300 65 88 44; web: www.tmvc.com.au. 20 clinics in Australia, New Zealand and Thailand.

South Africa
SAA-Netcare Travel Clinics PO Box 786692, Sandton 2146; fax: 011 883 6152; web: www.travelclinic.co.za or www.malaria.co.za. Clinics throughout South Africa.

Health

Switzerland
IAMAT (International Association for Medical Assistance to Travellers) 57 Voirets,
1212 Grand Lancy, Geneva; web: www.sentex.net/~iamat

First-aid kit
A simple medical kit might including the following; also remember sufficient
quantities of any prescription medicine:

- antiseptic
- wound dressings (Band-aids)
- suncream
- insect repellent; malaria tablets; impregnated bednet
- aspirin or paracetamol
- antifungal cream (eg: Canesten)
- Imodium for mild stomach upsets
- Ciprofloxacin antibiotic, 500mg x 2 (or norfloxacin) for severe diarrhoea
- antibiotic eye drops, for sore, 'gritty', stuck-together eyes (conjunctivitis)
- condoms or femidoms
- water purification tablets
- hypodermic needles in case you should need a blood transfusion or any other
  kind of injection

Practicalities

Malaria

There is a risk from malaria (predominantly plasmodium vivax and plasmodium falciparum in the south of Afghanistan) between May and November below 2,000m (which includes Kabul at 1,800m). The recommended prophylaxis is chloroquine and Paludrine (proguanil). These tablets are generally well tolerated and should be started one week before travel, whilst you are away and completed four weeks after leaving the malarial area. The main stay of preventing malaria is to avoid getting bitten, The female *Anopheles* mosquito that transmits the disease flies between dusk and dawn. Therefore it is wise to wear cover-up clothing, apply insect repellents containing the chemical DEET (eg: Repel brands) and ensure that your accommodation is as mosquito-proof as possible. Even taking every precaution is no guarantee that you will not contract malaria, so travellers should be vigilant for high fevers (38° or more) anything from seven days into the trip for up to a year after your return. If you have a fever and feel unwell in that time, then you should seek medical help as soon as possible.

Rabies

Beware of petting animals you don't know; rabies is a city-wide problem. Rabies is carried by all mammals, but in Kabul is most likely to be from dogs and is passed on to man through a bite, scratch or a lick of an open wound. You must always assume any animal is rabid (unless personally known to you) and seek medical help as soon as possible. In the interim, scrub the wound with soap and bottled/boiled water

Health

then pour on a strong iodine or alcohol solution. This helps stop the rabies virus entering the body and will guard against wound infections including tetanus.

If you intend to have contact with animals and/or are likely to be more than 24 hours away from medical help, then pre-exposure vaccination is advised. Ideally three doses should be taken over four weeks; contrary to popular belief these vaccinations are relatively painless!

If you are exposed as described, then treatment should be given as soon as possible, but it is never too late to seek help as the incubation period for rabies can be very long. Those who have not been immunised will need a full course of injections together with rabies immunoglobulin (RIG), but this product is expensive (around US$800) and may be hard to come by. Another reason why pre-exposure vaccination should be encouraged in travellers who are planning to visit more remote areas. Tell the doctor if you have had pre-exposure vaccine, as this will change the treatment you receive. And remember that, if you contract rabies, mortality is 100% – and death from rabies is probably one of the worst ways to go!

In Kabul

People new to exotic travel often worry about tropical diseases, but it is accidents that are most likely to carry you off. Road accidents are very common in Afghanistan, so be aware and do what you can to reduce risks: try to travel during daylight hours and refuse to be driven by a drunk. Listen to local advice about areas where violent crime is rife too.

TREATING TRAVELLERS' DIARRHOEA

It is dehydration that makes you feel awful during a bout of diarrhoea and the most important part of treatment is drinking lots of clear fluids. Sachets of oral rehydration salts give the perfect biochemical mix to replace this fluid, but any dilute mixture of sugar and salt in water will do you good. Quantities are approximately a four-finger scoop of sugar with a three-finger pinch of salt in a glass of water. A squeeze of lemon or orange juice improves the taste and adds potassium, which is also lost in diarrhoea. Drink two large glasses after every bowel action, and more if you are thirsty. These solutions are still absorbed well if you are vomiting, but you will need to take sips at a time. If you are not eating you need to drink three litres a day plus whatever is pouring into the toilet. If you feel like eating, take a bland, high-carbohydrate diet. If the diarrhoea is bad, or you are passing blood or slime, or you have a fever, you will probably need antibiotics in addition to fluid replacement. A single dose of ciprofloxacin (500mg) repeated after 12 hours may be appropriate.

Travellers' diarrhoea

Stomach upsets are the biggest health problem visitors to Afghanistan face, so don't drink the water or eat food that you're not sure of. Generally, even if the cook does

Health

not understand basic hygiene, you will be safe if your food has been properly cooked and arrives piping hot. The maxim to remind you what you can safely eat is:

PEEL IT, BOIL IT, COOK IT OR FORGET IT.

This means that fruit you have washed and peeled yourself, and hot foods, should be safe, but raw foods, cold cooked foods, salads and fruit salads which have been prepared by others, plus ice-cream and ice, are all risky. And foods kept lukewarm in hotel buffets are often dangerous. If you are struck, see below for treatment.

Water sterilisation

It is much rarer to get sick from drinking contaminated water but it happens, so try to drink from safe sources. If you can't get hold of bottled water, then you'll need to purify water for drinking. To do this, it should be brought to the boil, or passed through a good bacteriological filter or purified with iodine; chlorine tablets (eg: Puritabs) are also adequate although theoretically less effective and they taste nastier.

Medical facilities

Hospitals and clinics lack any capacity beyond emergency work associated with trauma surgery or diseases endemic to the region. There are, however, reports of good medical care from the Emergency Hospital, tel: +873 762 651 690. At the ISAF base on the Jalalabad road, there is also a German field hospital and a Czech hospital.

Just turn up for emergency treatment and things seem to move pretty fast. The German-run Malteser Hospital on the Police Academy compound just beyond the Intercontinental Hotel also has a good health service.

There is no blood-screening system in Afghanistan, and pharmaceutical products are often inferior or just plain out of date. Should you find yourself needing blood transfusion, be extremely cautious about accepting blood from an unknown donor. There are dentists out at the ISAF camps, but dentistry in the city's private practices is, in the main, still pretty rudimentary and based on tooth extraction for most dental problems.

In an emergency make sure your colleagues know your evacuation plan and have your health details to hand.

SECURITY AND SAFETY

All foreign nationals should register with their embassy on arrival in Kabul.

The **British Embassy** in Kabul has established a warden system but provides limited consular assistance. It is advisable for all British citizens working in and visiting Kabul to register with the Embassy at Karte Parwan, PO Box 334, Kabul; tel: +873 762 854 939; email: britishembassykabul@gtnet.gov.uk, kabulconsular@fco.gov.uk.

The **British Foreign and Commonwealth Office** issues travel advice (web: www.fco.gov.uk). For the foreseeable future the FCO is likely to be advising against 'all non-essential travel to Kabul and against all travel to other parts of Afghanistan'.

Trips to Pakistan, unless essential, are also advised against by the FCO, with the

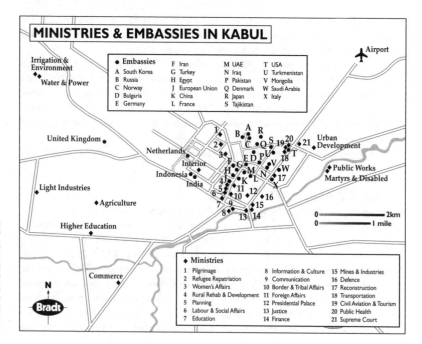

MINISTRIES & EMBASSIES IN KABUL

● Embassies

A South Korea	F Iran	M UAE	T USA	
B Russia	G Turkey	N Iraq	U Turkmenistan	
C Norway	H Egypt	P Pakistan	V Mongolia	
D Bulgaria	J European Union	Q Denmark	W Saudi Arabia	
E Germany	K China	R Japan	X Italy	
	L France	S Tajikistan		

Irrigation & Environment

Water & Power

Airport

United Kingdom

Netherlands

Interior

Indonesia

India

Light Industries

Agriculture

Higher Education

Commerce

Urban Development

Public Works

Martyrs & Disabled

0		2km
0		1 mile

N

Bradt

◆ Ministries

1 Pilgrimage	8 Information & Culture	15 Mines & Industries
2 Refugee Repatriation	9 Communication	16 Defence
3 Women's Affairs	10 Border & Tribal Affairs	17 Reconstruction
4 Rural Rehab & Development	11 Foreign Affairs	18 Transportation
5 Planning	12 Presidential Palace	19 Civil Aviation & Tourism
6 Labour & Social Affairs	13 Justice	20 Public Health
7 Education	14 Finance	21 Supreme Court

Practicalities

War on Terror continuing and tensions between India and Pakistan over Kashmir boiling.

For the latest **US advice** on travel to Afghanistan check the State Department web pages: www.travel.state.gov/Afghanistan.html; and for the latest travel warning check www.travel.state.gov/Afghanistan_warning/html.

If you're a real tourist (and there were at least two reported group tours in 2002), you're one of the first in Afghanistan since the hippy trail in the 1970s. Otherwise you'll be coming for work or visiting friends who are working in Kabul.

If you're visiting Afghanistan by yourself it would be wise to check in with a group and make friends quickly wherever possible and let people know of your movements.

Your personal security and safety should be your main concern whilst in Afghanistan and it is worth taking some time to prepare yourself and do the necessary research and attend safety training. Once in Kabul keep in touch with as many people as you can for details of the latest security situation.

Curfew in Kabul was lifted in November 2002 for the first time since the fighting for control of the city started at the beginning of the 1990s.

Generally, there is a great, friendly atmosphere in Kabul. As a visitor you are likely to become the centre of attention very quickly if you stop for a drink or a kebab on the street.

Be extra careful walking or driving around at night, as electricity in the city is not reliable. The streets are dark and obstacles appear to jump out at you. Beware of the uncovered manholes and storm ditches.

SECURITY AND SAFETY
The United Nations issues a pocket card for its staff with security information for emergency incidents in Afghanistan:

Dos
Do remain calm
Do contact a UN Security Officer or the Kabul Radio room immediately
Do remove yourself from the incident area
Do report the incident with the following details:

- Initiate your call on the radio with: 'EMERGENCY, EMERGENCY, EMERGENCY – SECURITY INCIDENT'
- State your call-sign/name (Who)

Practicalities

There are reports of muggings and robberies and international organisations have had computers and laptops stolen from offices; cars have been broken into outside restaurants and office safes broken into. But generally the main parts of the city seem safe. If you hire a taxi driver for the day, don't leave any belongings in the car when you get out to take pictures, and be aware that the service may be unreliable.

- Type of incident (What)
- Exact location (Where)
- Time of incident (When)
- Number of UN casualties (if known)
- Any assistance required (Ambulance/De-mining/ISAF)

Don'ts
Don't panic
Don't go to the site
Don't remain in the area
Don't use the radio until the radio channel has been reopened

Listen to the common channel for further instructions.

The main worry is the countrywide security situation, the continuing War on Terror and faction fighting between Afghan warlords. Whilst the International Security Assistance Force (ISAF) patrols Kabul regularly, there have been bomb incidents (September 5 2002: 30 people killed outside the Ministry of Information and Culture), political assassinations, bombs and explosives found in petrol tankers and cars coming into the city, and missiles fired into Kabul (as recent as April 2003).

Security and safety

FIVE POINTERS ON SECURITY

We've also spoken to a number of security gurus based in Kabul. Here are five pointers from 'Shaft', who worked for a major humanitarian NGO in Afghanistan:

Only you are responsible for your safety. Your actions will determine your future.

Health People working under pressure must keep themselves in excellent physical condition. You must allow time for relaxation, even if this means putting off important work. Get regular periods of leave because the physical affects the mental.

Conduct Avoid behaviour likely to arouse suspicion. Cameras, binoculars and tape recorders should be used with discretion and only after the necessary permission has been granted.

Official property When faced with an attacker whose main purpose seems to be looting rather than physical harm, **do not put the lives of the staff in jeopardy** over protecting organisation equipment.

Keep your head down If there is danger avoid the instinct to see what is going on, do not expose yourself and do not move unless you're going from a place of greater danger to a place of lesser danger.

The advice is to take extra care and keep in touch with developments. Areas where foreigners gather such as Chicken Street, restaurants and the UNICA Guesthouse are considered to be potential targets.

Most of the UN agencies, NGOs and media groups have their own safety and security guidelines for operating in Afghanistan. Many employ ex-military personnel who advise on work in the field and accompany staff on travels around the country.

Whatever you're doing in Afghanistan and whomever you're working for, you will need to ensure you or your organisation prepares properly and briefs you on security and safety.

If you're working in Afghanistan for an organisation you'll have to obey its security rules (eg: using radios at all times and travelling in a minimum of a two-vehicle convoy). You or your organisation may not be able to implement a full security plan like the major organisations, but it would be worth checking what others are doing, attending the regularly held security meetings (see below) and devising your own plans for evacuation.

Certainly consider packing a 'grab' or 'go' bag with basic supplies and equipment that is always by the door and can be snatched up should you have to leave immediately.

We experienced two serious earthquakes in Kabul in early 2002. The second, the stronger of the two, happened at 19.00, cut out the city's electricity supply and plunged wobbling buildings into total darkness. As a general rule, always make sure you know where your nearest exit is. Afghanistan is an earthquake-prone country.

Security and safety

Security for NGOs and journalists on worldwide operations has become a major concern over recent years with many organisations sending their staff on specialised training courses, such as those offered by Centurion Risk Assessment Services (web: www.centurion-riskservices.co.uk): 'Centurion is the world's leading risk assessment training company providing practical hostile-environments and first-aid advice and instruction to journalists, emergency and humanitarian aid workers and business people working in a hazardous region'.

There are a number of regular security briefings in Kabul that you'll be able to attend if you work for an NGO:

ICRC NGO security briefing	Thursdays at Shahre Naw, ICRC HQ: 08.30
UN NGO security briefing	Saturdays at UNDP compound: 14.00
ACBAR NGO security briefing	Mondays: 10.00

Emergency numbers
City police patrol tel: 020 118; emergency police tel: 020 210 1341
City fire department on duty call tel: 020 230 0304; fire chief tel: 020 230 0308

Mine awareness
The potential danger of wandering off the beaten track in Kabul cannot be over emphasised. After more than 20 years of war, the Afghan countryside is littered with unexploded mortar rounds, bombs, rockets, landmines and thousands of rounds of ammunition – some never fired, some duds.

Practicalities

Afghanistan is considered the most heavily landmined country in the world. Soviet forces fighting in Afghanistan placed most of the bombs during the 1980s. Before the American-led war against terrorism started the United Nations estimated that as many as ten million landmines were buried in Afghanistan. However, that number has now increased after US military planes dropped unexploded cluster bombs in Afghanistan in the push to rout the Taliban at the end of 2001.

It is estimated that a single landmine costs as little as 30 cents to make, yet the cost of finding and removing a single bomb can be up to 100 times that figure. By virtue of their cheap cost, millions of landmines have been scattered across the country and, because of the high cost of de-mining, remain there still.

On July 30 2002 Afghanistan signed up to the Convention on the Prohibition on the Use, Stockpiling, Production and Transfer of Anti-Personnel Mines and on their Destruction. It is estimated that 150 to 300 people are injured or killed every month due to mines or unexploded ordinance (UXO).

Handicap International Belgium (HIB), Qali Fatullah, House 104, opposite the Zarghoona High School (tel: 070 27 7314; email: mineawareness@handicap.org) runs mine-awareness courses for aid-workers and journalists, with 3–4 sessions per week for up to 20 participants (09.00–11:00, 14.00–16.00). Sessions are in English, Dari and Pashto and are also held in Kandahar, Jalalabad, Herat and Mazar-i-Sharif. For more details call in at HIB.

According to statistics published by HIB:

FATIMA'S STORY

It takes two men five and a half hours to clear 3m² of a minefield. There are more than ten million mines in Afghanistan spread over 824km². The hidden killers cause more than 100 deaths and injuries every month.

Nineteen-year-old Fatima Abrahim is one of those victims. She lost her right arm and left leg after treading on a mine as she played with other children in a field behind her house when she was ten. Her brothers and sisters ran screaming back to the house, her friends ran away; only Fatima's mother ventured into the minefield to rescue her daughter.

Fatima was taken to the small local clinic where her severed limbs were dressed with temporary bandages. The next day, she set out on what she says was the most excruciating journey of her life: a three-hour drive to Herat City and the nearest hospital. Fatima's older brother had died from a landmine explosion while she was still an infant. Despite her terrible injuries Fatima survived, but her recovery was to be a painful ordeal spanning more than four years.

At the hospital doctors amputated her left leg at the knee. Three days later after the first signs of gangrene began to show they took off four fingers from her right hand. However, her whole hand became infected and a few days later the surgeons operated again. This time her hand was amputated at the wrist. The poor healthcare in Herat hospital led to Fatima getting tetanus and the infection again spread up her arm. Six weeks after her first operation, Fatima's arm was amputated just below the shoulder. The operations were costly and Fatima's parents were forced to sell their land and home to pay the bills.

Three months later Fatima was finally able to return to her village where she started learning to walk again, but it was clear something was wrong with her amputated leg. As time passed it became more and more painful. After four years the doctors told her they would have to operate again: the bone was still growing. This time they amputated at the mid-thigh level.

Amazingly Fatima fought back from her injuries and aged 15 she married. At 16 she became pregnant.

'It was very difficult for me to carry a child with only one leg. I spent most of my pregnancy sitting down,' she says. 'I gave birth to a daughter, but after five months she died of dysentery.' Shortly afterwards Fatima's husband repudiated her, blaming the child's death on her disability, and they divorced.

Fatima now lives alone with her elderly parents whom she supports by working as a secretary for one of the international NGOs. They have no other source of income. Fatima cooks and cleans and does the shopping, although, 'People stare at me when I go shopping, and sometimes make rude comments.'

Fatima has lived almost half her life as a landmine victim; she says she has accepted her fate, but every now and then the anger still surfaces.

- More than 730km² of contaminated land makes Afghanistan the most heavily mined country in the world.
- There is another 500km² of battlefields littered by UXO and/or landmines.
- 150 to 300 people are injured or killed by mines or UXO every month.

De-mining has cost some US$666 million since the UN Mine Action Program for Afghanistan was started in 1989.

WHAT TO TAKE

Amazingly you can buy most things in Kabul; China is after all a neighbouring country. But you should come with a good torch, first-aid kit (see page 64), lipsalve, sunglasses, batteries and films for your camera, good walking shoes and warm clothes, sleeping bag, mosquito net for summer months and a small rucksack to use in an emergency.

Women should be aware that sanitary products such as tampons are virtually unavailable in Afghanistan and should come with enough supplies for the duration of any stay. A good short-wave radio or Worldspace digital receiver would also be a good idea.

MONEY AND BANKING

The currency is the Afghani (AFA). In March 2003 there were 50AFA to the US$, though the currency has fluctuated in early 2003 from between 45 to 57AFA to the US$.

There are no restrictions on bringing money into Afghanistan though there is a US$10,000 limit when leaving Pakistan.

The new Afghani came into circulation in the last few months of 2002. Prior to this, the exchange rate for the old Afghani had fluctuated between 30,000–50,000 Afghanis to the US$ and the highest note was a 10,000 Afghani. Afghanis in the north, printed by Uzbek warlord General Dostum, were also different and worth less. Over the last few years different warlords printed their own money in different former Soviet republics and the National Bank had no control over the currency.

In late 2002, 2,400 staff were employed in a massive money-shredding mission as old Afghanis were replaced with the new ones. Newly minted Afghanis are now commonplace and legal tender throughout the capital and the notes are in circulation in the provinces as well.

The new currency, aimed at creating financial stability, was launched on October 7. The World Bank assisted with the operation which involved shredding, drilling, or burning the old bank notes, the exact method depending on the technology available in different parts of the country. Helicopters were deployed to distribute the new notes to all the outlying areas and bazaars. The devaluation saw three noughts knocked off the old denomination. Thus 10,000 Afghanis (20c) became 10AFA; 100,000 Afghanis (US$2) became 100AFA etc. The new money replaced an estimated 15 trillion Afghanis in circulation, much of that printed illegally.

The National Bank (Da Afghanistan Bank) has set up a system for dollar bank accounts with a minimum of US$1,000 for opening an account with a chequebook

Money and banking

and an initial charge of US$50 (further charges are minimal). But otherwise you will have to travel with cash. Credit cards are not accepted anywhere.

Dollars can be used everywhere though most people on the street will prefer to be paid in Afghanis.

The money market is well worth a visit and most currencies can be changed. The traders there are infamous, even during Taliban times, for being able to get the latest exchange rates on their satellite phones.

COMMUNICATIONS
Telephone

The country telephone code for Afghanistan is +93.

The old telecommunication networks in Afghanistan are either non-existent or terribly run down. But things are improving in the major cities with a new GSM mobile-phone system being rolled out across the country.

In the summer of 2002 the Afghan Wireless and Communications Company (AWCC, web: www.afghanwireless.com) started a mobile-phone GSM system in Kabul that is being expanded across Afghanistan. (At the time of going to press the mobile-phone service was available in Kandahar, Herat and Mazar.) Throughout 2002 the central post office in Kabul was full of people buying mobile phones and top-up cards. Previously unheard ring-tones became a familiar sound and SMS text messaging took off across the city. The lines are surprisingly good and the cost cheap, though there have been periods of chronic congestion.

It costs 56 cents a minute to call the US and Canada, 58 cents a minute to call Europe and 64 cents to call Pakistan. Local calls cost 10 cents a minute. A significant saving on the old Sat phone!

AWCC local GSM mobile phones and top-up cards can be bought at the airport, central post office, Intercontinental Hotel, the AWCC office at the Ministry for Communications in the centre of Kabul (the ministry is the highest building in Kabul and as such is an unmistakable landmark), the Popo'Lano restaurant and other shops in the city. A SIM card costs US$130 and a handset costs US$120. Top-up phonecards can be bought for US$20, US$50 and US$100.

AWCC GSM phones begin with 070 followed by six figures.

Some of the old digital numbers do operate in Kabul and they begin with 020 followed by seven figures (internationally you'd dial +93 20 followed by the seven figures). The old five-figure analogue landline numbers are becoming redundant though some of them do still work.

To call most United Nations offices in Kabul you'll probably be ringing an Italian number or a New York number.

Most international organisations have satellite phones and GSM phones.

Internet

A number of internet cafés are springing up around the city which means you won't be landed with huge satellite phone bills any more. UN agencies and most NGOs now have constant internet access in their offices rather than standing out in the

Communications

garden trying to get a connection speed of 19Kbps from a satellite. But for most Afghans internet access is too expensive.

Aina Net Club At the Media and Cultural Centre next door to the Ministry of Planning and across the street from the Ministry of Foreign Affairs. Surfing costs US$4 an hour for internationals and non-members (there's a special membership scheme for Afghan journalists).

AWCC internet Café Downstairs in the Intercontinental Hotel: US$5 for an hour and US$3 for half an hour; open 07.00–21.00; tel: 070 82 0304

CHA Net Café At the Gallery of Fine Arts and Traditional Afghan Crafts on Cinema Zainab Rd: US$3 an hour, open every day 08.00–17.00 except Saturdays; tel: 020 220 0101; email: artgalery@cha-net.org; web: www.cha-net.org

Frough Net Café This place is a little further out from the centre of town on Matba-a St by Char-Rahi Macrorayon in the Soviet era Macrorayon 2 district. It's also a little cheaper than others. Run by Imal, it opened late in March. Currently open 06.00—21.00, the place has plans to offer 24-hour service.

Gandamak Lodge 5 Passport Lane. Free unlimited internet access for lodge guests wishing to connect their laptops.

Global Guesthouse Immediately off Flower Street behind big green gates: US$4 an hour.

Mustafa Hotel Café As you enter the hotel on your left: US$5 an hour and the chance to connect your own laptop and enjoy good fruit juices, coffee and sandwiches. Open '07.00 to very late'.

THE POST OFFICE IN KABUL

Kabul currently boasts the uncertain distinction of being home to the most underused postal service in the world. The main post offices in the central city areas are empty echoing halls with barren counters, and very bored-looking staff. This said, once a customer crosses the threshold, faces literally light up in delight at the prospect of performing a postal transaction. The two main Kabul post offices are situated next to the Interior Ministry in Interior Ministry Road, Shahre Naw and on Pashtunistan Square respectively. Postcards to almost every destination cost 12 Afghanis to send. Stamps for letters less than 10 grams in weight will set you back 14 Afghanis for the US, 15 Afghanis for Europe, 14 Afghanis for Australasia, 12 Afghanis for Pakistan, and 13 Afghanis for China, Africa and India.

The cost of sending a letter increases, obviously, with weight and the heaviest package the Afghan postal service will accept is a parcel of 1kg. Opening hours are from 08.00–15.00 every day except Fridays. The postmaster was a little coy when asked how long it would take for a letter or postcard to arrive. After an animated exchange with his colleagues, the consensus was delivery would take anywhere between six days and two weeks. For stamp collectors, the post offices are worth a visit for the stamps alone. Most of the designs in current use still date from the 1980s.

Communications

PACTEC Wazir Akbar Khan, Street 12. An internet café for 'approved NGOs' as certified by the Ministry of Planning. US$4 an hour; open Sat–Wed 08.00–16:00; Thu 08.00–12:00, closed Fridays; 1 hour 15 minutes costs US$5. You can also buy a Pop3 PACTEC email address for US$20 a month.

Park Net Café Ansari Square on Shahre Naw Park, part of the Park Residence. US$4 an hour. The signs in the window say they are open 24 hours a day but several after-hours visits have convinced us that this boast is merely a marketing gimmick. The place is well and truly shut after dark. However, you can connect your own laptop here; tel: 070 28 4144; email: park_net_café@hotmail.com

Courier services

DHL (web: www.dhl.com) Wazir Akbar Khan, Street 10, House 310; tel: 070 27 6362/63, 020 210 1891; email: kbl_hdesk@af.dhl.com. Open 08.00–18.00 every day. There's also a DHL office at the Mustafa Hotel and at Bagram airbase. DHL have daily flights to Afghanistan.

Federal Express (web: www.fedex.com) Karte 3, Khai Street, House 326; tel: 070 28 6028/29, 020 250 0525. Open 08.00–18.30, closed Fridays.

TNT (web: www.tnt.com) Turabaz Khan Crossroads; tel: 070 27 6503, 020 220 0266. Open 08.00–17.00, closed Fridays.

MEDIA

English-language newspapers in Kabul are pretty much restricted to two publications: the *Kabul Times* and the *Kabul Weekly*. Both have interesting insights to Kabuli life and some stimulating gossip as well. The papers are available from street sellers at traffic lights and cost around 10 Afghanis. Other newspapers will have a few pages of English in them.

Hamid Iqbal Co Ltd, Street 14, Number 4, in Wazir Akbar Khan, tel: 070 27 7629, can deliver international publications to your door, eg: subscribe to *Time* (US$8 a month) and the *International Herald Tribune* (US$90 a month).

The Hindokush News Agency at House 3, Muslim Street, Shahre Naw, distributes a daily news bulletin in English, Dari and Pashto for US$90 a month. Contact Najibullah Said, the director, tel: 070 28 0988.

The state-run Bakhtar Information Agency also distributes a daily news bulletin in English for US$200 a month. BIA is based at the Ministry of Information and Culture. Contact Mr Tawhidi the BIA director, tel: 070 27 9176.

For visiting journalists there are many press conferences held in the city. Regular UNAMA and ISAF briefings take place according to the following schedule:

UNAMA press conferences Thursdays and Sundays at UNAMA Compound B: 10.00.
ISAF press conferences Every day at ISAF HQ, opposite US Embassy: 09.30.

Tune your radio to 89.0FM and you'll get the BBC World Service in English mixed in with the Dari and Pashto services of the BBC. Remember to listen for the English news on the half hour.

Satellite TV is a must for anyone staying for a significant length of time. You'll see satellite dishes made out of Coke or hairspray cans and other amazing designs; they

Media

are cheaper than their fibre-glass, imported equivalents. You should also bring a good short-wave radio with you or a World Space Digital Receiver radio.

Radio in Kabul

107.5 FM	Radio Andernach	104.9 FM	BFBS
89.0 FM	BBC World Service	102.4 FM	BFBS 1
89.5 FM	Radio France International	104.9 FM	BFBS 2

For Afghans, radio has always been the main source of news and information with the BBC, Radio Free Afghanistan and Voice of America (VOA) being the most popular. There are about 20 TV and radio stations across the country and this number is likely to increase as international organisations help various groups set up their own stations.

On International Women's Day, March 8 2003, the Voice of Afghan Women radio station was launched in Kabul (91.6 FM). A radio station is also being set up by some Afghan Australians which will feature Indian, Iranian, Western and Afghan music (Radio Arman, 98.1FM). UNESCO is also working with Kabul University on plans for a student radio station.

The national broadcaster in Kabul, Radio TV Afghanistan, is run-down and stuck in the Soviet dark ages with a huge staff producing very little programming. The Taliban destroyed much of the film archive. But brave archivists did manage to save some of the material by smuggling it out of the station or building false rooms behind hollow walls. Most Afghans will watch satellite TV or inexpensive pirated VCDs, though it must be noted that the live coverage of the historic Loya Jirga in June 2002 attracted huge audiences.

There have been numerous battles between the TV management (controlled by the Northern Alliance) and the more liberal Ministry of Information and Culture over having women presenters on TV and women singing. The screening of popular Bollywood and Western films has also been a point of contention. Interestingly, TV in Kandahar, the home of Taliban leader Mullah Omar, very quickly allowed women and foreign films to be seen on TV, but a more hard-line control in Kabul has remained.

The deputy minister for information and culture tells a story that a foreign journalist once complained that there was no Indian film on TV on a Sunday night and that this had to be the latest round of censorship. The minister replied, 'Sunday night is for American films.'

ELECTRICITY

220 volts; AC 50Hz. A constant, stable electricity supply is a real problem in Kabul. Most offices and guesthouses have to run generators for much of the day. Plug sockets are European-style two pins, but you can buy any type of adaptor and extension cable imported from China. Beware: laptops and mobiles phones can have serious difficulties with the electricity supply and batteries never fully recharge.

ACCOMMODATION

There are numerous guesthouses in the city and a number of hotels, all of varying standards. More details are in the *Where to stay* section on pages 107–18.

Our advice for first-time visitors arriving in Kabul with no contacts or accommodation is this: head straight to the Mustafa Hotel. The manager Wais Faizi, who returned from America, knows the city well and can organise a car and translator for you. The hotel is popular with journalists and within walking distance of Chicken Street and Flower Street where you can buy all your souvenirs and supplies. The hotel also has a good café and internet terminals.

The Intercontinental Hotel, which is unfortunately almost 30 minutes from the city centre, is struggling to get back to normal but there is a good internet café there.

EATING AND DRINKING

You'll be eating a lot of lamb kebabs and *Kabuli pilau*, rice with raisins and carrots (the national dish) and *mantu* (spicy dumplings). Look out for *ashak*, a delicious pasta dish, reputed to be the forerunner of ravioli. This is a special dish that Afghans often prepare for big occasions and feast days and everyone looks forward to it materialising on the table!

You'll always be offered tea, especially green tea (*chai saps*), at any meetings, homes or whilst you're shopping on Chicken Street. Make sure you try the delicious Afghan bread, *naan*, lightly leavened and delicious when hot.

In the summer the colourful markets are full of mouth-watering displays of fruit and vegetables, but a thorough washing of them is advised before you bite in to any succulent-looking, unpeeled varieties.

For imported food and drink, ISAF and most NGOs are using the Supreme Food Service (tel: 070 27 4949; web: www.supreme-foodservice.com; email: kabul@supreme-foodservice.com) on the Jalalabad road out of Kabul, just before the Italian ISAF base. All kinds of food and drink are available, most at duty-free status. You no longer need to establish a minimum US$500 account as there's now a supermarket attached to the main warehouse. That said, the supermarket is more expensive and often lacking in certain items, so it is worthwhile ordering in advance and buying in bulk.

On Flower Street you can buy most of your supplies, such as bottled water, cornflakes, tinned food, chocolates, cheese and cigars, but it will cost you and you'll have to do a lot of bargaining with shopkeepers who really won't budge a cent on a US$4 pack of cornflakes.

On Butchery Street in Shahre Naw you can choose your own cut of meat from the hanging carcasses in the shop fronts: a word of warning, however: this is not for the faint-hearted.

It is also worth mentioning that Afghanistan, as an Islamic state, is a dry country. According to Islamic law Muslims are forbidden to drink any alcohol. Clearly, it is impossible to buy alcohol in any Afghan shops or restaurants. The country's most popular drinks are tea, *chai* and fizzy drinks such as cola and lemonade. While

RUSSIAN BEER AND VODKA IN KABUL

Dominic bought 24 large cans of Russian Baltika St Petersburg Number Eight beer in March 2002 for an extortionate US$190, which works out at a dollar for every percent of alcohol. In the same shop two Afghans were debating whether to buy gin or whisky. The beer was hidden at the bottom of a freezer below Sprite, Coca-Cola and tinned military rations from the various international forces in Kabul. Even bacon omelette was available. Later in the year he bought a bottle of Russian vodka, still with the USSR stamp on it. It had been hidden in a cellar for more than 15 years. It was the best vodka he'd tasted, even after spending a year in Siberia!

alcohol is available to the expatriate community through Western food outlets such as Supreme Foods on the Jalalabad Road, it should be bought, transported and consumed with extreme discretion. Never, ever consume alcohol in the streets or any other public places for that matter.

For information on eating at restaurants, cafés, hotels and guesthouses see the listings on pages 118–27. Most of the internationally run guesthouses offer imported food on their menus and even full English and Irish farmhouse breakfasts.

CULTURAL DOS AND DON'TS
Tipping and baksheesh

Tipping is, of course, how many Afghans make some extra money from foreigners, especially as official salaries are so low (around US$40 a month). You should certainly consider giving a dollar or two to someone who helps you, such as the man who let you into the Royal Family Mausoleum, or the person who showed you around the zoo. But if you've negotiated a fee with a translator or driver then there's no need to tip extra unless you've had excellent service.

You'll hear the word *baksheesh* shouted at you from every direction. Unfortunately, once you get your money out you'll be surrounded and it can get quite intimidating and depressing (especially with women in *burqas* asking for money). Favourite spots for the 'baksheesh brigade' are at traffic lights and in every single traffic jam.

Outside the popular restaurants there are usually a number of children, women and people with disabilities asking for money.

In the Wazir Akbar Khan area of Kabul, where many foreigners live, you'll often see children offering to polish your shoes or selling newspapers (and this guide) and a number of clearly destitute people asking for money.

Of course what you give and when is a personal decision. Just be aware of your safety and the fact that the more often you give the larger the group of people gathering outside your home will become.

For the children, sweets, pens and notebooks are also in demand. They will always ask for your pen.

FROM THE ORIGINAL PRESS RELEASE ON 'THE SURVIVAL GUIDE TO KABUL'
A Guide to Kabul That Helps The City's Street Kids
Jude Barrand reporting from Kabul, 12 September 2002

A guide to Kabul co-written by Caritas Press Officer, Jude Barrand is helping put a few dollars in to the pockets of a handful of street sellers in the Afghan capital.

The Survival Guide to Kabul is a 16-page pocket reference tool for all city-dwellers. It lists hotels, restaurants, and all the sporting and cultural events in the city. An exclusive article by the region's most famous author, Ahmed Rashid, (the bestsellers Taliban and Jihad are his best-known books) has also boosted the small pamphlet's success.

'As the first 500 copies rolled off the press we realised we needed to find an effective way of getting our guide to Kabulis and expats alike,' explains Dominic Medley from Internews, an NGO that trains journalists worldwide.

'The most obvious solution was the street children who hawk the city's many weekly newspapers down at the main traffic intersection in the commercial hub of Kabul. We get wonderful distribution through the children, and they get to keep the money they make by selling the guides.'

The children have been quick to catch on to the money-spinning venture and every morning come to the Internews office in Kabul to pick up their daily quota of copies to sell.

Armanullah is 12 and has been selling papers on the streets of Kabul ever since the city's printing presses started up again after the fall of the Taliban. Before that he scavenged in rubbish tips for food.

'I am happy to be selling this paper,' he says of the guidebook. 'I get to keep all the money I make and some foreigners especially give me a lot.'

Up at the Intercontinental, Kabul's biggest hotel, foreign journalists wander through the lobby holding copies of *The Survival Guide to Kabul*.

On gently interrogating two reporters from the main Japanese television network, it emerges they bought their guides from the street children. Each paid a dollar for their guide.

Donal O'Reilly, the Kabul Office Programme Manager for Caritas Member Organisation, CRS, was one of the many accosted by the street children at the traffic lights.

His reaction was to pick up his phone and call the authors to congratulate them on the positive off-spin to bringing out a guide:

'You've got a real income generating scheme going here,' he laughed. 'The kids are out here selling the guide to anyone they can. It looks like they are making a killing.'

Cultural dos and don'ts

We found the original version of *The Survival Guide to Kabul* our way of helping. We gave the guides to the kids for free and they sold them for as much as they possibly could. We also invited the children in for cans of Coke so we could tell them about selling the guide and ask them about their lives.

Dress

For men and women visiting Afghanistan it is best to dress down and avoid being noticed. Remember the more inconspicuous you are, the safer you are.

Most agencies will have guidelines at their arrival briefings for their staff. Clothing for women is more prescribed than that for men. Foreign men in the city can wear pretty much what they would at home. Shorts however are the exception: Afghan men never show their legs. Any Western man showing his legs would draw huge amounts of attention. It's a fact that you never see joggers in the city.

Some Western women visitors do wear a veil over the head; it depends how you feel. The all-encompassing *burqa* is not worn by non-Afghans and many Afghan women in Kabul are discarding it now.

Legs and shoulders, however, must be covered at all times. Anything that fails to cover all the limbs will be considered provocative and the woman in question will find herself the subject of extremely unpleasant attention.

Some people, especially outside Kabul, will consider even three-quarter-length sleeves offensive.

Men and women may wish to consider wearing the traditional, long knee-length shirt and pyjama trouser ensemble known as the *shalwar kamiz*. It is comfortable and very practical for all kinds of work and travel. In the summer the loose cotton garment is very cool and is more acceptable to local populations for travel into the provinces.

Outside Kabul take care with local sensitivities. In Kabul, visiting women needn't wear a headscarf but in Herat, for example, it is essential.

The state of the roads and streets in Kabul mean practical walking shoes are the best.

It is customary to remove your shoes before entering a mosque or holy shrine. Women should ensure their heads are covered before entering.

Cultural dos and don'ts

AFGHAN PROVERBS (IN DARI)

Yak roz didi dost. Digar roz didi brodar
Friendship grows into brotherhood
Literally: One day you see a friend. The next day you see a brother

Har guli bi khar neest
No one is perfect
Literally: No rose is without thorns

Har amal axol amalley dorrad
Every action has a reaction
Literally: A tree does not move unless there is wind

Yak tir du budanah
To kill two birds with one stone
Literally: One arrow, two finches

3

The evocative Afghan capital has seduced new arrivals since time immemorial. Its beautiful setting in the Kabul River Valley, ringed by towering mountains on all sides, has captured the hearts and minds of some of history's most illustrious figures. Despite the destruction of recent decades, that allure lingers still. The very word 'Kabul' summons up history-book tales of epic adventure, intrigue, diplomatic machinations, battles, oriental opulence, barbarous rulers, decadent princes, enlightenment, splendour and conquest.

Since September 11 2001 the intrigue has taken on a new meaning. Afghanistan became the centre of the War on Terror. Kabul suddenly became the focus of international attention. The world's media descended on the city. Major UN and humanitarian agencies moved in to begin the long process of reconstruction, a task that will demand a lasting commitment if Kabul and Afghanistan are to have any chance of a brighter future after so many war-ravaged years.

There's been a settlement in Kabul for at least 2,500 years. Since then, competing powers and forces have been drawn irresistibly to the city to lay claim to its riches and the strategic position it offers, particularly for the control of the Khyber Pass to the Indian subcontinent.

Today Kabul is a city of massive contrasts. The neat and newly spruced-up semi-suburban enclave, Wazir Akbar Khan, to the north of the city is the adopted stamping ground of NGOs, diplomats and journalists. During the Taliban regime it was home to many of their officers and Arab supporters. West Kabul, however, once home to gracious avenues, sumptuous villas and the magnificent Darulaman Palace, is

AHMED RASHID'S KABUL

Since the 1960s no city has witnessed as many dramatic changes and as much destruction as Kabul. For former King Zahir Shah, who returned to his capital in early 2002 after nearly 30 years in exile, the changes were extremely emotional and apparent. The last time Zahir Shah saw Kabul, the city may have been an international diplomatic backwater, but it was also a thriving, bustling town where the elite had a hectic social life. The Cold War was at its height and both the Soviet Union and the US were mildly courting the Afghan monarch with economic aid. The Americans built airports and roads in the south of the country, while the Soviets did the same in the north. Often their contractors would meet up, for example when the Kabul-to-Kandahar highway was built.

Only after the coup that toppled Zahir Shah in 1973 did the coup-maker – his cousin Mohammed Daud – turn wholeheartedly to the Soviets for military training for his army and the disgruntled Americans abandoned Afghanistan. By then Kabul was the centre of late hippiedom as Westerners travelled to India and stopped off at Kabul for cheap hashish and the ability to live on next to nothing. Wine and cognac were cheap, courtesy of adventurous Italians who set up a wine factory in Kabul based on the grapes grown in the Shomali plain. The wine was exported to Pakistan, Iran and the Soviet Union. There was a vibrant teahouse culture where men and women students from Kabul University would discuss politics and the latest fashions. The most popular place was the Café in Pashtunistan Square opposite the central post office where the dating game was played furiously after 16.00 and it was all a matter of seeing and being seen.

Kabul's élite would then move to the Hotel Kabul and newly constructed Intercontinental Hotel where foreign bands offered live dance music. Pasta and sauerkraut and sausages were available in German and Italian restaurants, which were run by hippies who had decided to stay on. Tourists from neighbouring Pakistan and Iran would flock to Kabul for weekends in order to shop for duty-free foreign goods, see Indian movies, drink and dance.

The Communist revolution in 1978 changed the city as the two warring factions of Khalq and Parcham battled each other in the capital and the first wave of exiles – mostly royalists – escaped to Pakistan and later the West. A year later the Soviet invasion brought in tens of thousands of young Soviet troops who initially acted in the same manner as their Western counterparts – smoking cheap dope, shopping for carpets and Western electronic goods in Chicken Street and hanging out in cafés.

Then the war started in earnest as the Mujaheddin launched guerrilla attacks from Pakistan. The Soviet troops were restricted to their barracks. Girl students took part in anti-Soviet demonstrations in the city and were brutally suppressed. At the same time tens of thousands of Kabulis took part in a massive literacy campaign launched by the Soviets and many students were shipped off to the Soviet Union to further their education and to be indoctrinated in communism.

However, for many women the war was in a sense a liberating experience. As Kabul's male population were forced into the Afghan army, women took over many jobs. Eventually some 40% of jobs in government ministries, schools and hospitals were taken up by women – many of them from poorer classes who were for the first time going to work dressed in skirts and high heels.

Although living conditions were hard there was no major fighting around the city until the Mujaheddin captured Kabul in 1992. That led to the start of the brutal civil war which lasted a decade and destroyed large parts of central Kabul as well as creating wave upon wave of refugees leaving the city until there were hardly any educated or technically qualified people left. The fighting around Kabul came to an end only when the Taliban captured the city in 1996, bringing with them relative security, but also harsh Islamic measures that destroyed the vitality of the city's population.

Kabul quickly became a ghost town; women became invisible and social life outside the home next to impossible. Cinema halls were shut down, the radio played only religious speeches and cafés were shut down. The only place where social interaction took place was the mosque.

The revival of Kabul's social life after November 2001 has been dramatic in the extreme. Within days of the retreat of the Taliban and even though the majority of people were desperately poor, the bazaars were once again thronging with people, women appeared in the streets for the first time and music blared in every bazaar. As education and clinics and hospitals revived with the help of international aid agencies, women were back at work in large numbers.

The future of the city now depends on funds being made available for genuine reconstruction work – providing water, sewerage, electricity and a telephone system and rebuilding the battered roads of the city. Kabulis' expectations from the international community are enormous and fulfilling them will not be easy and will take time.

Ahmed Rashid is author of the bestsellers 'Taliban' and 'Jihad' and correspondent for 'The Daily Telegraph' and the 'Far Eastern Economic Review'. This article was first published exclusively in the street edition of 'The Survival Guide to Kabul' in autumn 2002. He has established the Open Media Fund for Afghanistan to support the print press in Afghanistan. Donate by contacting JoAnne Sullivan of Internews in Washington, tel: +1 202 833 5740; fax +1 202 833 5745; email: jsullivan@internews.org; web: www.internews.org).

Kabul City

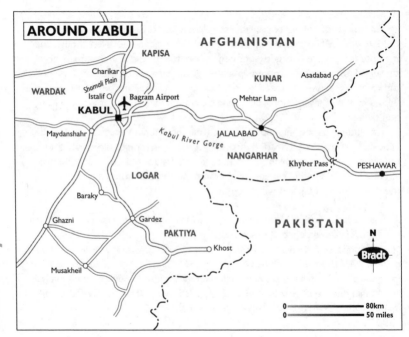

AROUND KABUL

AFGHANISTAN

KAPISA

Charikar

WARDAK

Shomali Plain

Istalif

Bagram Airport

KUNAR

Asadabad

Mehtar Lam

KABUL

Maydanshahr

Kabul River Gorge

JALALABAD

NANGARHAR

Khyber Pass

PESHAWAR

LOGAR

Baraky

Ghazni

Gardez

PAKTIYA

Khost

PAKISTAN

N

Bradt

Musakheil

0 ———— 80km

0 ———— 50 miles

destroyed probably beyond repair. The area was completely flattened during the Mujaheddin 1992–96 fighting when as many as 50,000 people lost their lives.

But the bazaars along the river still bustle with activity as people strive to make a living for themselves. The city now is crowded as people have returned from exile and the international community has moved in. Traffic jams block the city for much of the morning up to 10.00; beggars and street children line the traffic jams asking for any amount of small change.

Business is thriving. Guesthouses and restaurants have opened with amazing speed. Hotels like the Hotel Kabul and the Intercontinental are being refurbished. The Kabul Museum, the National Gallery and the National Archives are all being restored and prepared for opening. The historic Babur Gardens are being laid out again, with a restaurant and coffee bar being renovated.

Kabul was once a cosmopolitan city, taking advantage of its pivotal position as a Central Asian crossroads. It could yet regain that status.

GETTING AROUND

Travelling around Kabul is relatively easy and safe – it is just time consuming and loud as well, with car horns going off all the time. Take deep breaths on your journey and don't expect to get anywhere on time. Also be aware that street names and house numbers are not easy to spot and many people just don't know what many significant landmarks are called as names have been changed repeatedly by successive regimes, causing city-wide confusion.

In the last year traffic has increased dramatically. Taxis, buses and bicycles are everywhere, as are international 4WDs. One taxi driver estimated there to be 40,000 taxis in Kabul. Traffic jams are now both common and long every day in the morning between 08.00–10.00 and in the afternoon around 16.00.

You'll be able to flag down a taxi easily and you're likely to be sharing with one or two other people.

Outside Kabul travel needs to be taken with caution and advice sought on the latest security situation. Roads are not maintained, driving is chaotic and the motto among most Afghan drivers seems to be 'get there first, dead or alive'. International agencies report that driving accidents are the main source of death and injury for their staff.

If you're working with the UN, then under their regulations you probably won't be allowed to drive a car. Most NGOs employ drivers for their staff though many foreigners do prefer to drive themselves, especially outside working hours.

Remember, never leave the road in a part of the city you are unfamiliar with, even when turning or pulling over; landmines are still a roadside hazard.

Car hire

The ATO (see page 42) can get you a car into the city for US$10, a car for a day for US$40 and a translator for US$40 a day. The ATO can also organise a car for return journeys to Kandahar (US$200), Herat (US$340), Mazar (US$200), Bamyian (US$150) and Paghman (US$20).

WHERE TO STAY

Most international organisations working in Kabul have their own guesthouses for their employees. Others are put up in the numerous guesthouses in town. These are all private houses converted into bed and breakfasts of varying standards and services. If you're arriving for the first time without any accommodation arranged you're probably better off heading straight to the Mustafa Hotel. The taxi driver at the airport will know where it is, there's a good vibe there, lots of journalists and other foreigners and Wais, the owner, is a real Mr Fix It and can get a translator, driver and car set up for you. It's also right in the centre of town and just a short walk from Chicken and Flower streets where you can buy all your souvenirs and supplies (including bottled water).

Hotels

Intercontinental Hotel (200 rooms, only 30 in use; 4th and 5th floors being renovated into executive rooms) On the outskirts of the city heading into West Kabul; sat phone: +873 761 469690 or local tel: 020 220 1320.

Probably the best-known hotel in Kabul, this is the place for all the international conferences, and a temporary home to many journalists, diplomats and Afghan government ministers (many of them chose to live here when they returned to Kabul after the fall of the Taliban). One drawback is that it's on the outskirts of town heading into the destroyed part of West Kabul so you'll have to face a lot of long Kabul traffic jams if you base yourself here. It was opened in September 1969 and built by a British company. Returning Afghans from

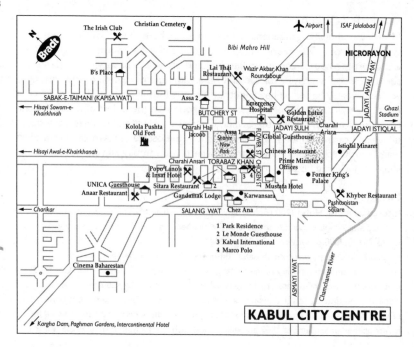

Kabul City

The Irish Club
Christian Cemetery
B's Place
SABAK-E-TAIMANI (KAPISA WAT)
← Hisayi Sowom-e-Khairkhnah
← Hisayi Awal-e-Khairkhanah
Kolola Pushta Old Fort
← Charikar

Bibi Mahro Hill
Lai Thai Restaurant
Assa 2
BUTCHERY ST
Charahi Haji Jacoob
Charahi Ansari
Popo'Lano's & Insaf Hotel
UNICA Guesthouse
Sitara Restaurant
Anaar Restaurant
Gandamak Lodge
SALANG WAT
Chez Ana

Airport
ISAF Jalalabad
MICRORAYON
Wazir Akbar Khan Roundabout
Emergency Hospital
Golden Lotus Restaurant
JADAYI SULH
Charahi Ariana
JADAYI ISTIQLAL
Ghazi Stadium
Assa 1
Shahre Naw Park
Global Guesthouse
Istiqlal Minaret
FLOWER ST
CHICKEN ST
Chinese Restaurant
TORABAZ KHAN
Prime Minister's Offices
Former King's Palace
1 3 4
Mustafa Hotel
Karwansara
Khyber Restaurant
Pashtunistan Square
ASMAYI WAT
Chanchamast River
JADAYI AWALI MAY

1 Park Residence
2 Le Monde Guesthouse
3 Kabul International
4 Marco Polo

Cinema Baharestan

↙ Kargha Dam, Paghman Gardens, Intercontinental Hotel

KABUL CITY CENTRE

N
Bradt

the 1970s remember coming up here for burgers and chips as a special treat as children. The hotel is slowly being restored to its former glory and is currently under South African management. An encouraging development is the new à la carte Bukhara Restaurant that opened in March 2003 and serves Indian cuisine. Next door, in the newly refurbished Bamyian room, there's a delicious and very popular buffet brunch served up on Fridays, Saturdays and Sundays, 11.00–15.00. At US$8 a head it's worth every cent.

There's also a new fitness centre at the Intercontinental Hotel opened in April 2003 (see *Fitness centres*, page 132). There's also a swimming pool, tennis court, ping-pong and billiard tables, sauna, barber and other shops and an Ariana Airlines office. The hotel is ideal for conferences and has hosted numerous events since the fall of the Taliban. The ballroom seats 400 for dinner, or 600 for a conference. Check your email at the AWCC Internet Café in the basement with its high-speed connection, printing and scanning facilities. Open 07:00–21:00 daily for US$5 an hour and US$3 for half an hour. It will cost you US$1 to print an A4 page. *Rates: US$157–231 (deluxe), US$74–137 (standard) a night.*

Mustafa Hotel (50 rooms) In the centre of town close to Chicken Street and Flower Street where you buy your souvenirs and supplies; tel: 070 27 6021; email: mustafa_hotel@hotmail.com
For first-time visitors to Kabul the Mustafa is the place to head for. The hotel is popular with journalists. Kebab night is on Thursdays on the roof terrace. The refurbished restaurant serves good pizzas and there's a pool table, darts, DVD room and basketball court. In 2002 the hotel organised a football league and there are plans for a baseball league in 2003. The

Where to stay

Mustafa Hotel Café serves good fruit juices and sandwiches and the AWCC Internet Café allows you to connect your own laptop as well as surf on the ten desktops. The hotel manager is Wais Faizi who featured in the July 2002 *Newsweek* article *The Exiles Return*. Wais also features in Christina Lamb's *The Sewing Circles of Herat*: 'We quickly nicknamed Wais "the Fonz of Kabul" for his New Jersey accent and fast-talking "tell me whaddya want, Wais can geddit" manner. A short but powerful-shouldered man of 31 with a jutting chin and passion for Al Pacino movies, he was a former body-building champion and knew everyone in town.' Check out the original *The Survival Guide to Kabul* promo on the staircase as you enter the Mustafa Hotel and the painted Al Pacino movie posters around the hotel.
Rates: US$35–45 a night.

Hotel Kabul (73 rooms) Pashtunistan Square next to the Ariana Airlines office.
This 50-year-old, large Soviet-style hotel has been under renovation since late 2002 when the Aga Khan bought the property. Before then this once cosmopolitan, jet-set hangout was in a terrible state. Years of neglect gave it a shabby external air, but following the Aga Khan's visit to Kabul in mid-November 2002, the word is that the place is about to undergo a dramatic and much-needed transformation, perhaps resulting in a hotel similar to the Aga Khan's luxury Serena Hotel in Islamabad. It is expected that the hotel will be open to guests in 2003.
Rates: The US$40–80 a night charged at the old Hotel Kabul will no doubt increase.

Kabul International (14 rooms) Just before the Marco Polo Restaurant and Chicken and Flower Streets: tel: 020 220 1124; email: kabulinternational@hotmail.com

Billed as 'your own cosy place to stay'. Has some well-appointed rooms with TVs, fridges, AC and intercom system. There are two toilets and showers per floor. Kabul International is also a restaurant with Indian chefs.
Rates: US$50–80 a night including breakfast.

Park Residence (55 rooms) On Shahre Naw Park next to the old Czechoslovakian Embassy; tel: 070 28 0576.
All the rooms have en-suite shower, fridge and TV. There's a parking area and a large garden, which in the summer of 2002 the manager Naqib said was ideal for 'live music'.
Rates: US$30–75 a night.

Hotel Spinzar (36 rooms) Next to the Ministry of Information and Culture, Asma-yee Wat; tel: 070 27 4983.
This is a large five-floor hotel in the centre of town. The 1970s' concrete building has seen better days. There is still a flavour of a more cosmopolitan past with a main hall and a terrace. However, the building is now dated and tatty and rooms are rudimentary and bland. Windows were blown out during the bomb explosion on September 5 2002 (which killed 30 people) outside the hotel by the Ministry of Information and Culture. The restaurant serves only Afghan food but, when large parties don't overwhelm it, it can be good.
Rates: Nationals pay US$5 for a single room and US$6 for a double room. Expatriates are charged US$20 and US$35 respectively.

Where to stay

Insaf Hotel (43 rooms) In the Shahre Naw part of the city.
This hotel is currently being refurbished but promises VIP rooms, an internet café and coffee bar. It is also home to the very popular Popo'Lano Italian restaurant.
Rates: US$35–50 a night.

Guesthouses

There are numerous guesthouses, most of them in the Wazir Akbar Khan (WAK) area of the city (see also page 117). Most guesthouses in WAK are pretty much the same, though furniture, fixtures and fittings do vary. Charges range from between US$30–60 a night (always negotiate, especially for long stays). Rooms usually have two to four beds in them. Dining and lounge facilities include satellite TV.

If you're staying for a short period of time and are on a budget then you probably won't be interested in luxury. But for long stays try to get your own room with a bathroom nearby and negotiate accordingly. It will always work out cheaper than renting a full house in WAK (prices per month were US$3,000–10,000 or more in 2002, cash in advance).

Assa There are two guesthouses in this brand new chain in Shahre Naw. Assa 1 is located just off Flower St, House 140, St 5; email: assa.kabul@hotmail.com. Assa 2 is House 9, Muslim St; tel: 070 27 4364, 27 6579.
The Assa guesthouses are the latest in fair-quality accommodation in Kabul. Facilities include satellite TV in the lounge and large, comfortable rooms. Assa 2 even has a swimming pool

that they assure customers will be filled for the summer; however, it is currently little more than an extremely large birdbath.
Rates: US$50 a night.

Bs Place (6 rooms) Qali Fatullah; tel: 070 27 6416; email: b@place.as.
Run by Matt Woods, an Australian, Bs Place is more expensive than other guesthouses but has a more modern feel than the guesthouses in WAK. The décor is well thought out, and there's a good menu. The lantern-lit garden is great here in the summer and very popular (you'll need to book for dinner as it does get full). There's also a small gym around the back of the main house.
Rates: US$75 a night, US$65 for longer stays, including breakfast.

Chez Ana, Media Action International (12 rooms) Passport Lane; tel: 070 28 2699.
This place is run by Ana Pongrac from Croatia and NGO Media Action International that was set up by long-time Afghanistan journalist Eddie Girardet. Ana has featured in Croatian newspapers, *Croatian Cosmopolitan* and on Croatian TV. Lunch costs US$3 and dinner US$8; non-residents are welcome to book in advance for meals.
Rates: US$35–50 a night including breakfast.

Gandamak Lodge (17 rooms) Number 5, Passport Lane; tel: 070 27 6937.
Renowned BBC cameraman Peter Jouvenal set up The Gandamak Lodge. Osama bin Laden apparently used to meet one of his wives here. This place takes you back in time with its collection of guns, historical pieces and good furnishings. Gandamak is open for breakfast

ARRIVING IN KABUL FOR THE FIRST TIME
Dominic Medley

I arrived on February 17 2002 on board the UNHAS flight from Islamabad. It was cold, raining and the airport was chaotic. Soldiers were everywhere, some of them barely 16 years old, and all armed with a variety of weapons and AK47s. The Afghan minister of civil aviation and tourism, Dr Abdul Rahman, had been assassinated on board an Ariana plane just a few days before. The first story out said angry Haj pilgrims had killed him. It later became clearer that it was a political assassination. The minister's certificate of airworthiness for the Ariana planes from January 2002 is posted on the Ariana website. I arrived with three colleagues. Two of us didn't have visas. Our passports were taken and we were assured that the necessary documents were obtainable at the Ministry of Foreign Affairs. Not a happy feeling losing your passport the moment you arrive. But everyone was going through the same procedure, even UN staff. Afghanistan's embassies around the world were not operating at the time.

The lights at the airport weren't working but luckily I had a torch handy to search for our luggage. We lost some equipment, an AP cameraman lost two boxes of tape. We all thought it had been stolen. Instead it just hadn't been put on the UN flight in Islamabad. The equipment arrived the next day.

Our group walked out of the airport. Haj pilgrims and Afghan soldiers were everywhere, though surprisingly, compared to the Balkans, not an international soldier in sight. A swarm of young Afghans speaking English approached us shouting 'taxi', 'guesthouse', 'you need translator'. We opted for two of them, Hamid and Yama, who took us to the Faisal Guesthouse. Luckily we'd already heard about the Faisal in Islamabad. Negotiations for the cost of the car continued for the whole journey. Negotiations for the cost of the guesthouse lasted throughout the evening. But I was into Kabul for the first time in my life, three months after the fall of the Taliban. It was the beginning of a nine-month adventure in 2002, which was to continue in 2003.

I'm happy to say that the following day we did get our passports back. We managed to track down the various officials at the Ministry of Foreign Affairs, the NGO Department and the Planning Department, and other departments I forget, to get the necessary letter to present at the airport, then pay US$30 (complete with scrubbed out Taliban regime passport stamp), retrieve our passports and then get down to the Passport Office for the latest official three-month multiple-entry visa. Obtaining an extension visa in the country relies on knowing the system and making sure you find the 'responsible person'. Otherwise it's a day of headaches.

(US$5) and they do candlelit dinners in the garden in the summer. Book before midday and for US$20 (US$15 for guests) you'll enjoy a three-course meal. Drinks will cost you extra. Each room has free unlimited internet access. The Gandamak Lodge is also expanding into new premises across the road with en-suite rooms and a new pizzeria.
Rates: US$45–65 a night including breakfast.

Global (13 rooms) Just off Flower Street and Cinema Street before the Assa 1 Guesthouse; tel: 070 28 1907; email: edward.dean@globalpsw.com.pk.
The Global Guesthouse is run by Global Risk Strategies. The rooms are decorated with the finest Afghan furniture, including big double beds with white counterpanes and matching curtains. Its location in a large compound just off Flower Street makes it central but very restful. There's a walled garden area with a volleyball court (open invitation on Friday afternoons). Other facilities include a fully catered dining room, internet terminals, weights room, TV room with DVD, terrace and security. The Global Café opened in February 2003 and is open daily and in the evenings.
Rates: US$50 a night including meals.

Helsinki (6 rooms) On the way to the airport; tel: 070 28 4305; email: osmankhaliq@hotmail.com.
The Helsinki bills itself as a Scandinavian guesthouse 10 minutes' drive from the city centre on the way to the airport. There's a large spacious living room with a fireplace.
Rates: US$50 a night including breakfast.

Karwansara 117 Interior Ministry Road, opposite the Interior Ministry, next to the Malalai High School; tel: 070 29 1794 or 29 5520.

Karwansara is a guesthouse and restaurant complex in the same vast compound, each one in a separate building, both with echoes of colonial grandeur. The guesthouse is in an imposing, but slightly less charismatic building than the restaurant. The style and décor, as with the restaurant, are impeccable, but the rooms are chilly and some are very small. A gym and internet facilities are being built on to the guesthouse. There's also a branch of the London Afghan Travel Centre here.

Rates: US$50 a night.

Le Monde (13 rooms) House 7, near the Sitara Restaurant in Shahre Naw; tel: 070 28 0751, 28 0741; email: lemondegh@hotmail.com.

Two rooms have en-suite bathrooms and there are kettles provided in every room.

Rates: US$45–70 a night including breakfast.

Guesthouses in the Wazir Akbar Khan (WAK) area

Ajmal Wali Street 10, No 140; tel: 070 27 7657

Everest Street 10, No 192; tel: 070 28 1277

Faisal Street 15, No 27; tel: 070 27 4696

Faisal Bilal/German Street 15, No 73; tel: 070 27 4808/070 28 1413

Haseeb Street 13, No 556; tel: 070 27 4986

Hendokush Street 10 Z, No 9; tel: 070 27 9558

Where to stay

House 150 Street 10; tel: 070 27 8734
Marvellous Street 10, No 214; tel: 070 27 5519
Popo'Lano Street 10, No 3; tel: 070 29 1483
Rose Valley Street 14, No 3; tel: 070 28 9019/070 27 4590
Shamal Street 13, No 452; tel: 070 27 8601
Silk Route Street 10, No 138; tel: 070 27 5800
Sultan Street 10; tel: 070 27 7374
Taj Mahal Street 15, No 128; tel: 070 27 5830

Other guesthouses
Naween Kolola Pushta; tel: 070 22 4411/070 29 1588
Park Shahre Naw; tel: 070 27 5728
Pearl Continental Shahre Naw; tel: 070 28 3706

WHERE TO EAT
Restaurants
In Kabul you can eat almost anywhere – there are kebab stalls on every corner. Restaurants were slow to open after the Taliban fell but there are now several places that serve good foreign and Afghan food and no doubt more will begin to open, mainly serving the large international community. You'll often see richer Afghans celebrating birthdays at the Golden Lotus or Khyber Restaurant.

Consider your security when visiting some restaurants. In February 2003 the

British Agencies Afghanistan Group (BAAG) issued a warning in one of its regular bulletins: 'In the light of possible hostilities in Iraq, international staff should be aware that, if they are attending parties and consuming alcohol, they may be under observation. A number of restaurants, including Bs and the Indian are considered to be "soft" targets from the security point of view and DfID, (the British Government development and aid agency) has already placed a ban on its own staff using these.' At the end of April 2003 the Irish Club was temporarily closed after the UN and other organisations banned their staff over security concerns.

One of the best ways to enjoy Afghan food and hospitality is of course to accept an invitation to dinner with an Afghan family.

The following is a by-no-means-comprehensive list of places to eat in Kabul.

Anaar House 6, Street 4, Kolola Pushta, behind the UNICA Guesthouse; tel: 070 28 4315, 070 29 1857. The Anaar offers a wonderful, warm dining experience. It's located down a lantern-lit alleyway. The restaurant reception and dining rooms are hung with beautiful Afghan carpets. In fact all the décor is local. A magnificent, carved wooden doorframe in the far restaurant room is a fantastic work of art. In this room, diners can sprawl on Afghan cushions and eat from low-level tables, but elsewhere there is seating and at the far end of the seated dining room there is a vast fireplace. The cuisine is described as Indian, Chinese and Thai. Indeed the restaurant is co-owned by an Indian and Afghan who have brought their culinary experiences to play here very successfully. The Thai green curry is particularly good. The place is open for lunch 11.00–15.00 and for dinner 19.00–23.00 (though one

Where to eat

friend of the authors was at a party until 03.00). Dinner costs around US$12 a head. There is no alcohol served here, but you can bring your own as long as you are discreet about consumption and request permission from the management first. According to one diner it provides 'the most relaxing and intimate restaurant yet in Kabul'.

Bs Place The guesthouse in Qali Fatullah; tel: 070 27 6416; email: b@place.as. The food is more expensive than many of the other places listed, but the menu boasts Thai green curry and shrimps flown in from Dubai. Pizzas cost US$6–14 and a pepper steak costs US$7. The menu also includes Greek salad, hoummus, steak and chocolate fudge cake. During the winter months, there's a typical Afghan *sandaly* room. (A *sandaly* is a heated low table with a thick table cloth. Food is placed on top and the diners sit as snug as bugs with their legs under the table.) Outside, there's a lovely garden with trees, lanterns and a flower shop. It's better to book tables and food in advance. You can buy alcohol with your meal, or bring your own. Bs also has a free delivery service for customers in their immediate area ordering take-away.

Chinese Restaurant Ansari Square, Shahre Naw just before the Chicken and Flower Street junction; tel: 020 220 1618. There's space here for 60 people downstairs and 40 people upstairs with three private rooms with tables, sofas, TVs and karaoke systems. There's a free salad buffet and the usual Chinese food. A hot and sour soup will cost you US$1.50, sweet and sour chicken US$6 and beef in oyster sauce US$6. The restaurant has permission to serve alcohol but not to Muslims. Open 11.30–23.30.

Delhi Darbar 1 Muslim St, Shahre Naw; tel: 070 27 7566. The Delhi Darber has just moved to new premises. There's a US$6 buffet at lunch and dinner with good popadums and great garlic naan bread. Delivery is available.

Gandamak Lodge 5 Passport Lane; tel: 070 27 6937. Gandamak Lodge is open for breakfast (US$5) and dinner. Book before midday and for US$20 you can enjoy a three-course meal of mostly imported food and the cheese plate. Drinks will cost you extra. A menu for one night in March 2003: appetizer: quiche Lorraine with tomato chutney; main course: poached plaice with lemon-butter sauce, herbed risotto, stripped courgettes sautéed with balsamic vinegar; dessert: hot lemon-curd soufflé.

Golden Lotus Across from the German Embassy. The Golden Lotus serves Chinese, European and Afghan food. It opened in the early 1970s and was the first Chinese restaurant in Kabul. Surprisingly, the Taliban did not close it down, and the restaurant was one of the first to reopen early in 2002 after refurbishment, attracting a number of foreigners who have now moved on to the newer restaurants in the city. Prices are cheaper than other places but the food is very rice-based.

The Irish Club Opposite the NGO, FHI in Taimani, tucked away beneath Bibi Mahro Hill not far from Bs Place; tel: 070 29 6698. Open 07.00 until late, the Irish Club opened on St Patrick's Day, March 17, 2003 and instantly became a big hit in the city. Here you can find everything you would expect from a good Irish establishment, including a fully stocked bar, draught Guinness brought in from Dubai, and Stella Artois on tap. There's an Irish farmhouse breakfast for US$5 every morning. Lunch is a buffet meal and the evening meal à la carte with an international chef cooking up dishes ranging from Irish stew to a traditional T-bone steak. The owner is Irish-Australian, Sean McQuade, who has been working in Afghanistan for the past 11 years. The Mighty Quinn in Perth, Australia, is the sister bar to the Afghan set-up. There's a fabulous veranda here where you can get a cappuccino during the day and dance at night. Every so often there are Australian barbecue evenings where you buy a plateful of meat for US$6 and cook it yourself over the huge grill in the garden – with help if needed!

This club plans a membership policy. A full year will cost US$300, and monthly membership US$10. The favourable short-term pricing is designed for those on short contracts and volunteers in Kabul and, as the management freely admit, it's Irish logic. If you are in town for a matter of days you can pay a one-off entrance fee at the gate. The club also boasts an internet café, a satellite TV room, and a private room for up to 12 people. There are also limited guesthouse facilities, which are likely to be expanded. The bar has no fixed closing time. As the owner himself says, 'If there's a good crowd in, we won't throw them out!' Currently a room is around US$50 a night. The Irish Club also featured in *The Times* 'Travel' section on April 5 2003, together with a photo, thanks to the authors of this guide. *The Times* wrote: 'It's one of the key indicators that a city is back on its feet: Kabul now has its own Irish bar.'

Kabul International Just before the Marco Polo Restaurant in Shahre Naw; tel: 020 220 1124. The chefs from India serve a daily lunch and dinner buffet of curries for US$8 a head and promise Italian, Chinese, Mexican and continental food is on the way. There's a large roof terrace that should be a great hangout in the summer.

Kabul Restaurant Part of the Hotel Kabul with an attractive garden and terrace that once served a variety of food. The hotel is being renovated so we await developments there.

Karwansara Situated within the Karwansara Guesthouse compound, 117 Interior Ministry Rd, Next to Malalai High School; tel: 070 29 1794. The restaurant is being described by many of its habitués as simply the best dining experience in Kabul, thanks largely to its fantastic setting. The décor is beautiful and the views at night over the city lights on the hillside opposite are stunning. Karwansara is the old name for the travellers' inns on the Silk Route and the restaurant does justice to recreating some of that old atmosphere. There's a traditional cushioned Afghan area where you can stretch out and take *chai* and off the main seated areas there are little cushioned dens for those looking for greater intimacy. The menu is described as a mixture of Afghan and some Western cuisine. There is no alcohol served here, but you can bring your own as long as you are discreet about consumption and request permission from the management first. A meal for two costs around US$15. Perhaps the most attractive thing about this place is the fact that 50% of the profits from the venture go to running an orphanage housing 16 children (Khorasan House, a project of the Khorasan Charity Organization, which is a registered charity in the UK). The other 50%, says the management, goes back into the local economy. The Karwansara is run and owned by an Afghan woman who has returned home after 30 years in Britain, and is staffed front-of-house by a cheerful group of young waiters.

Khyber On Pashtunistan Square in the centre; tel: 020 210 1840. The Khyber is one of the many reminders of the city's heyday. Back in the 1960s this is where Kabul's cosmopolitan city dwellers converged for *chai* (tea) and coffee at the pavement café. Now tatty and dilapidated, the pavement outside is used for parking and the inside is used mostly as a conference hall. However, the Khyber does still do a popular buffet lunch. There are three kinds of food on offer, Italian, Chinese and traditional Afghan all for US$6 a head, not including drinks. The restaurant has seating for 150 people in the main hall and room for a further 45 in the second smaller salon. There is a third room at the back of the restaurant that is rather dark and dusty that can seat 130. Special parties can be accommodated provided the management is given advance warning. Ideally you should let the general manager, Satar Formoly, know a good three days in advance. The Khyber Restaurant only has a local landline so you may be better advised to drop around to make any arrangements in person.

Lai Thai Wazir Akbar Khan, Street 15, second road on the left, House 124; tel: 070 29 7557. Within days of opening in April 2003, the Lai Thai established a reputation for excellent food and service in a pleasant, tastefully furnished setting. The waiters and waitresses are dressed in traditional Thai clothes, the furniture has been especially designed in Pakistan and the attention to detail is visible in the décor, right down to the beautiful cutlery. The spring rolls (US$4 for a plate of four) are possibly the best outside Bangkok (where the chef and restaurant owner come from). Lalita Thongngamkam is the dynamic owner and has extensive experience of running restaurants. She has run similar establishments in Kosovo, East Timor and Australia and personally supervises all the cooking in the kitchen. There is seating for 40 people downstairs and for another 30 upstairs. A main course costs around US$7. The fried ginger chicken and coriander is superb, as are the deep-fried vegetables; the giant prawn soup at US$5 is simply mouth-watering. There is no alcohol available, but if you ask permission you are able to bring your own. The Lai Thai is open for lunch and dinner 11.00–22.00. The restaurant also runs a catering service for parties, office dos and any other special occasions. Lalita also runs a traditional massage service (see page 132). This is a serious health and beauty massage done by a professional masseuse using traditional techniques.

Popo'Lano Part of the Insaf Hotel in Shahre Naw; tel: 070 28 8116. Popo'Lano was one of the first restaurants to open in Kabul in the summer of 2002 and was probably the most popular restaurant among internationals. This Italian restaurant has a reasonably priced, good menu. Pizzas cost US$5, with take-away and delivery available. There's also a carpet and Afghan souvenir shop here. The manager is Abdullah.

Shandiz Iranian restaurant on Wazir Akbar Khan, Street 10; tel: 070 28 4026. The Shandiz opened in March 2003 and is one of the newest buildings in Kabul, serving Iranian food. Shish kebab with rice will cost you US$9. The Shandiz opens at 09.00 as a coffee shop, is open for lunch from 11.00–15.00 and dinner from 18.30–23.00. Delivery is available.

Other restaurants you might like to try are the **Marco Polo** and **Herat**, two typical kebab and rice restaurants. The Marco Polo is near Chicken and Flower streets. The Herat in Shahre Naw is an attempt at a fast-food restaurant with the guys running around in baseball caps. **Chief Burger** opposite the Cinema Park does a variety of fast-food and burgers. The **Sitara's Afghan Food Restaurant**, just off the park in Charahe Ansari, is promising to be a great place for Afghan food and currently has seating spaces for 500 people for conferences and seminars (Amnesty International held a press conference here in March 2003). To book a place, speak to Meraj on 070 28 0584. The **Khalid Restaurant**, just past the Emergency Hospital, is closed now but it used to be a typical kebab restaurant in 2002 and before that a cinema which was closed by the Taliban. There are numerous kebab and *mantu* stalls around the Cinema Park in Shahre Naw such as the **New York Restaurant**.

Where to eat

Cafés

Mustafa Hotel Café This little den provides a warm atmosphere on the ground floor of the hotel. There's a comfortable 'soft' area to sink into while you enjoy a good milkshake for US$2 and a variety of fruit juices. The internet café costs US$5 an hour. An outside courtyard café is due to open and a summer cinema season is to be inaugurated on the outdoor screen in 2003. Live musicians are also on the entertainment programme. This place, however, is well known as a popular haunt for Westerners and a warning was posted in February 2003 advising people to be extra careful when in the area.

FRESH JUICE

A number of great juice bars have sprung up along the main Shahre Naw Road opposite the Cinema Park. A stop here is cheap, refreshing and delicious and the choice is mouth-watering. Take your pick from a ruby-coloured pomegranate juice (*anaar*) or a bright orange carrot drink (*zardak*). There's also banana (*kela*), apple (*seb*), grape (*angur*), cherry (*gelass*) and melon (*kharbuza*) to name but a few – seasonal availability depending. The juice comes in a tankard-style glass. It is advisable to request that your drink comes without ice (contaminated water isn't purified by freezing) though it is unlikely you'll be offered any outside the hot summer months. At the time of writing a long, cool juice drink costs 20AFA.

Global Within the Global Guesthouse off Flower St and Cinema St there's a full menu of refreshments, drinks and espresso/cappuccino, music, and an outside, south-facing seating area. Global says the 'relaxing atmosphere will be a refuge from daily Kabul life and ideally placed for shopping, pre- and post-dinner drinks etc'.

A **Café Cappuccino** promises to open just beyond the Emergency Hospital and across from the CHA Art Gallery but in March 2003 they had a sign in the window: 'wanted, expert to make coffee cappuccino'.

SHOPPING

Just turn right out of the Mustafa Hotel, then walk for a minute and take the first right and you're on Chicken Street that leads into Flower Street.

Chicken Street is the Oxford Street (Rue St Honoré, Fifth Avenue or Via Condotti) of Kabul. This is where you come to shop! Small, single-storey, ramshackle buildings teem with silk scarves, *pakoul* hats (the type made famous by the deceased 'Lion of Panjshir', Ahmad Shah Massoud), carpets, jewellery, glassware, lapis-lazuli chess-sets and trinkets and baubles of every colour, shape and form imaginable! Eager shopkeepers will do their best to lure you in with their winning patter, but it's all good-natured. Prices are high (one carpet-seller we know of came down from US$300 to US$50 for a rug) so beware of the sharks and be ready to do some haggling.

Halfway down Chicken Street you can find the Habibi Book Centre, tel: 070 28 9577. Among other things, this small emporium sells newspapers from Pakistan,

Shopping

Time, *Newsweek*, and an interesting if somewhat restricted selection of English-language books.

Carry on into Flower Street. There you can find some pretty good grocery stores selling those home-brand luxuries like Earl Grey tea, Nutella, and Kellogg's cornflakes. A word of warning: the concentration of Westerners here has made Chicken Street a security concern. Do not linger.

For electrical goods go to Technology Street. Turn left outside the Khyber Restaurant. You get can mobiles phones and accessories at the Mobile Palace (tel: 070 28 1450) across from the Popo'Lano Italian restaurant. The Galaxy Store (tel: 070 27 6570, 27 9825) next to the Marco Polo restaurant sells TVs, satellite systems, mobile phones and accessories.

For traditional carpets, check out the old building next door to the money market. To get there, go across Kabul River on the Froshga pedestrian bridge.

Halfway down Flower Street next to the Marco Polo Blue Palace Store is the Asree Store and Bakery. This bakery sells French baguettes and doughy, white, leavened loaves. The raisin bread is excellent.

On Flower Street, next to the Asree Bakery, the Hollywood DVD Music and Video Store sells rip-off DVDs for US$1–2. The choice is pretty ropey. Action films and Bollywood epics are the favoured genre, but the selection is always being increased.

The women's bakery, run by the NGO Women for Women International, sells bread and cakes (tel: 070 22 4973). A small chocolate mud cake costs US$15 and *focaccia* bread costs US$2. The baking is done in partnership with the guesthouse Bs Place to help needy Afghan women learn new skills and earn some money. They'll be happy to test your own recipes and they welcome guest trainers.

The Popo'Lano restaurant at the Insaf Hotel in Shahre Naw has a bakery selling French bread, pancakes, lemon, chocolate and cheesecakes, croissants, tarts and Danish pastries.

For all kinds of sports equipment go to Kabul Sports and Afghan Sports and Toys next door to each other and across the road from the Popo'Lano restaurant in Shahre Naw. You can also try the little sports outlet next to the Chelsi Grocery Store on the corner of Flower Street.

For arts and crafts you can visit the **CHA Gallery of Fine Arts and Traditional Afghan Crafts** at House 76 on Cinema Zainab Road, just past the Emergency Hospital; tel: 020 2200101; web: www.cha-net.org. The **Afghan Handicraft Promotion Centre** opposite the Indian Embassy on the Interior Ministry Road also has crafts for sale.

WHAT TO DO

Admittedly, leisure time is not something most Afghans or foreigners working in Kabul will be thinking of. For most people, work is the order of the day as the efforts to reconstruct the country struggle forward. Nevertheless, there are some things to do which you could consider outside the long office hours and outside your guesthouse room – when time permits. Here are just a few ideas:

BUZKASHI

This amazing game, the national sport of Afghanistan, deserves a mention in this guide. Although the popular sport is played predominantly in the north of the country, provincial championships are held in Kabul from October through to November, with one-off matches being staged for special occasions ranging from weddings to Naw Rouz (New Year, celebrated on the first day of spring, March 21). The games usually take place on Thursday afternoons and Fridays.

The game is usually played by between 20 and 30 horsemen split into two teams, but this is by no means a definite rule. It has been known for hundreds, even thousands of horses and riders to take part. The aim is to get a decapitated calf weighing around 150 pounds to a heavily defended marked point and back again to the starting point. Each team takes turns in defending and attacking. The ensuing mêlée is exhilarating, death defying, skilful and brutal. Huge sums are exchanged as bets are placed on the outcome and the sport's champions are lionised by the people.

Sport

For sport there are **tennis and squash courts** at the old German Club (at the time of writing the club has been taken over by US management and changes are expected), the UNICA Guesthouse, the Intercontinental Hotel and the British Embassy.

The **swimming pool** at UNICA is popular (members only). The ICRC, Italian and French embassies (invitation only), and Intercontinental Hotel (guests only) also have pools.

The reopened Microrayon public swimming pool was very busy on August 19 2002, Independence Day, when the place was full of Afghan men. It cost 20,000AFA (50 cents) and the water was very cold and murky, leaving little to the imagination as to what was at the bottom.

There's **football** every afternoon in Shahre Naw Park with the Afghan All Stars (local kids having a kick around – boisterous but fun). The Mustafa Hotel ran a football league in 2002 and plans a baseball league in 2003.

There's usually **rugby** at the ISAF base across from the US Embassy on Fridays.

The **Hash House Harriers** in Kabul started in August 2002. The first meeting was on a Friday at the Intercontinental and cost US$3. Conservative clothing is a must for all runners.

Fitness centres and beauty parlours

There are a number of fitness centres around town, and Turkish baths and beauty parlours for women. Men and women should remember that even in a fitness context shorts are unacceptable. Both should work out in long tracksuit bottoms, and women should wear long-sleeved tops.

Gold Gym In the Soviet-era district Macrorayon 2, this is one of the more popular gyms with Afghans and internationals alike. It is visible from afar thanks to an imposing hand-painted poster of a superhumanly proportioned body-builder in a pair of very short red shorts. The gym is run by the former Afghan wrestling champion Bawar Hotaki and has 30 brand-new exercise machines which are mostly weights based. No Afghan women use the gym. Membership is 300AFA a month. Opening hours are 06.00–10.00 and 14.00–20.00. It gets very congested in the evenings.

Intercontinental Hotel There's a new fitness centre at the hotel (see page 107), open 06.00–21.00 daily. Monthly membership is US$80; members receive an ID card. The men's section has a barbell bicep bench, combination weight bench, stair stepper, and combination lat press, and the ladies' section has an exercise bike, treadmill and two exercise mats. There are separate shower and changing facilities. Currently the swimming pool is only open to men.

Rokhsar Beauty Parlour Flower St. This is one of the better beauty parlours in town; it is also slightly pricier. The all-women zone is a single room offering waxing, threading, make-up, hair styling, washing and cutting, manicure, pedicure and henna-ing.

Thai Traditional Massage Tel: 070 29 7557. The Thai massage service is offered by one of the women working at Lai Thai restaurant (see page 124). The traditional Thai massage incorporates acupressure and joint-loosening techniques, and is done through clothing. The expert masseuse, who has more than ten years' experience, uses her weight to manipulate the body; the end result purports to improve blood circulation, boost the immune system and flush out toxins caused by stress. Currently, the massage is done on a mattress on the floor in a small, furnished room above the restaurant, although the management plans to move the service to a more pleasant location in the coming weeks. One hour's massage is US$25. You need to book an appointment in advance.

Wahida Assa 2 Guesthouse, Shahre Naw; tel: 070 28 7360. Wahida runs a beauty parlour at this guesthouse, and also describes herself as a 'mobile beauty parlour' for women only at their homes. She only uses imported beauty products. Facial US$10, pedicure US$8, manicure US$7, haircutting, waxing and massages are just some of the beauty treatments she offers.

A professional massage is also available, by appointment only (tel: 070 28 8208), at **Ming Ming's**, off the Kolola Pushta main road pass the UNICA Guesthouse.

Culture and entertainment

The Aina Media and Cultural Centre, next door to the Ministry of Planning, has a lovely grass courtyard. In the summer big-screen **film showings and musical evenings** take place. There are also regular **exhibitions** at the centre. Every Tuesday night Aina has a film showing at 20.00.

There's **live music** planned in the outdoor courtyard at the Mustafa Café throughout the summer as well as a summer **cinema** season on the large outdoor screen. Check dates and times at the Mustafa Café.

Finally, consider **learning the local language** at a number of places or from private tutors. The Aina Media and Cultural Centre (tel: 070 28 4581) runs a

What to do

DRAWING THE AFGHANS
Jake Sutton

I started drawing in Kabul in February 2002. On my first day after arriving from Jalalabad I saw a British soldier in the Herat Restaurant and asked if I could spend some time drawing at the ISAF HQ. I went along the next day and had a meeting to explain my project. I wanted to record and document both Afghan people and soldiers of ISAF. I noticed that ISAF hired quite a lot of local Afghans to do many of the non-military jobs on the base. Something came as a shock when I did my first drawing of an Afghan. I looked at him after I had finished and thought he was 39 or 40 years old; as I always put the age next to the person's name, I needed to know. Well, through a group of people in the small crowd around us, someone kindly asked his age. I could not be more shocked and surprised: he was 20!

I had to take another look; how could this be so? Well, I put his name and age down, frankly not quite believing it. I looked around the small crowd to see who could be next. I looked at someone, he smiled, and I could see he was willing to be next. When I had finished again I asked his age, waiting to hear around 37 or 38. I was getting something wrong, very wrong: he said 21.

number of courses. Interlit (web: www.interlitfoundation.org), based in Peshawar, publishes books on learning Dari and Pashto, which are popular with

After drawing about six Afghan men, I realised my judgement of their ages was consistently out by about 20 years. It became clear to me as I did more and more charcoal drawings that something happens to the Afghan face. Life is hard, very hard, the air so dry and dusty, and this is reflected across their face, across their skin: it, too, is dry, and ages much faster than in the West. The Afghans have to be the nicest people I have drawn: they sit still so well, and they enjoy you taking an interest in them. The men have strong features. They live life out of doors, living off the land with little or no money, yet walking down a street in Kabul it's hard to find someone not smiling, joking, laughing, just enjoying life, freely shouting across the road 'How are you? How is your health? What's your name?' I have really had great pleasure in doing about 350 large charcoal drawings of people who are so rich in their friendship. From street-working children in Kabul to a farmer in Bamyian, they are all pleased you have visited their country and spent time with them.

Jake Sutton is a freelance TV cameraman and photographer who spent the end of 2001 and most of 2002 and 2003 in Afghanistan. Charcoal portraits by Jake are online at web: www.afghanistanportraits.com.

expats, and a book of Afghan proverbs. These books are available at the Intercontinental bookshop and elsewhere in Kabul.

What to do

Church services

There's a Roman Catholic Mass at the Italian Embassy at 17.00 on Sundays and feast days. Father Moretti will be more than pleased to see you.

WHAT TO SEE

There's a lot to see in the city, even if most of it is wrecked. Touring Kabul is best done on a Friday when the city is quieter. A three-hour trip will give you time to visit some of the must-sees such as the spectacular views from TV Tower Hill, the Darulaman Palace, Kabul Museum, the destroyed west of Kabul and King Nadir Shah's tomb.

Of course cameras and foreigners attract the *baksheesh* brigade but everyone is very friendly. Afghans love posing for photographs and digital cameras mean you can show the results immediately or print them out and deliver copies later (photographs as gifts are much appreciated). Always ask permission as well if you want to take photos. However, do remember that Kabul is one of the most mined cities in the world. Never wander off the beaten track.

No trip around Kabul is complete without Nancy Hatch Dupree's pocket guidebook, widely available at street bookshops or at the Intercontinental Hotel. Originally published in 1965, a second edition was printed in 1972. Five suggested tours around the city are laid out in detail with sights to see and maps to guide you. Needless to say, Kabul has changed dramatically in the last 30 years but the book gives an interesting insight into what the city was like. Eight tours for outside the city are also suggested. Most notable is a trip to Ghazni to see the minarets, though these days the 140km drive takes closer to four hours in a 4WD. The shopping section offers an interesting perspective of what Kabul used to be like. Though the city's skyline has changed, the accounts of the overflowing markets show that perhaps not that much has changed after all:

> The richness of Kabul's bazaars is legend: they are as fascinating today as they have always been. We recommend departing from this general guideline so that you may experience the pleasure of discovering a favourite bazaar or a unique 'find'.

West Kabul

The whole of West Kabul sums up the wanton destruction the city has seen. West Kabul used to be a huge residential area with the grand avenue leading to the Darulaman Palace and Kabul Museum. Thousands of people were forced to flee, however, as the rival Mujaheddin factions rained shells at each other across the avenues and villas from their strategic positions in the surrounding hills. As a result of that sustained shelling, the area was reduced to rubble and dust. Today it's a haunting reminder of Kabul's recent history, with the palace and the museum being the most striking evidence of the bitter legacy of war. Just beyond Kabul Zoo is a roundabout with the **Maiwand Memorial Column** in the middle. The completely destroyed surrounding buildings are what most TV crews have filmed over the years to emphasise the destruction of Kabul.

Kabul Museum

The Kabul Museum is in front of the Darulaman Palace and is undergoing extensive renovation with help from organisations like the British Museum and UNESCO. The museum was famous in Central Asia for its prehistoric to 20th-century collection, but over the last ten years 70% of the collection has been lost. Although the museum is closed, we did manage to get inside and meet the director and his deputy. The director, Mr Omara Khan Masoudi, who's worked at the museum for 24 years, showed us the rooms being renovated; most are for storage though he hopes exhibitions will open by the end of 2003. In the foyer is a magnificent huge black marble basin, surrounded in Islamic text, dating from the 15th century. Back then the basin would have been filled with juice for pilgrims to the Sultan Mir Wais Baba shrine in Kandahar. On the wall down the corridor is a 12th-century calligraphic frieze from Laskhar Gah. Opposite the frieze is a 12th-century reconstructed mosque, also from Lashkar Gah. There's a lovely 19th-century Arabic-style marble door that belonged to the royal family. In March 2003 the main corridor was full of old steel filing cabinets that used to house the museum's collection of 40,000 coins. Sadly all the coins, many dating from the time of Alexander the Great, have been looted.

The library has a collection of books, mostly stored in trunks. Fortunately, the Taliban didn't destroy many of the museum's books, but outside you'll see the ruined statues of lions and horses. The second floor of the museum was completely destroyed in a fire in the mid-1990s. In 1995 the museum did try and start the process of retrieving objects but then the destruction began again under the Taliban who destroyed around 2,000 pieces. The museum director says there's a huge job to be done to restore the museum and the collection. He's also worried that people are still looting Afghanistan's heritage. 'I'm sure there are some ancient pieces on Chicken Street, but we haven't checked,' he says, though he adds that most of the 'guns on Chicken Street are new and not ancient'. Mr Masoudi also says many of the museum's pieces are still in hiding.

Darulaman Palace

The palace, built by King Amanullah in the 1920s, is set into a small hill in front of the Kabul Museum, with the once impressive four-mile avenue – once lined with poplars and home to the former Soviet Embassy, schools and ministries – leading to it. Fighting from 1992 onwards destroyed the building but it remains one of the most impressive, albeit shattered structures in Kabul. The palace was used by King Amanullah and was later used as the Justice Ministry and Defence Ministry. The equally striking former Defence Ministry is on the hills behind.

Kabul Zoo

Kabul Zoo is a soulless complex and is not a great place for its inhabitants. In 2002 China donated two lions, two bears, two pigs and a wolf. In addition there are a number of other species including nine bears, jackals, birds, rabbits, eagles, wild boars, foxes, guinea pigs, monkeys, owls and six huge vultures. In total the

MARJAN THE LION

In January 2002 the most famous resident of Kabul Zoo, Marjan, the one-eyed lion and veteran of so much fighting, died. Marjan, the only lion in the zoo, was a gift from Germany 38 years ago and was estimated to be forty years old. Half blind and almost toothless, he'd survived all the fighting in Kabul, even in the 1990s when rival Afghan groups fought for control of the city and the zoo was on the frontline, in the direct line of fire from rocket attacks launched from the nearby hills. Marjan lost his eye when a Taliban fighter climbed into the lion's enclosure. The starving Marjan killed and ate the man, but the man's brother returned the next day for a revenge attack and threw a grenade into the cage, leaving Marjan blind and lame. In his last few weeks Marjan enjoyed a heated cage and plenty of food and medicine.

zoo has 116 animals and a staff of 60 to care for them. Conditions are poor but it is a popular place for Kabulis and up to 3,000 people will visit during a week according to the director Sheragah Omar who has worked at the zoo for nine years. A British animal protection group, the Mayhew Animal Home in London, ensures there is enough food for the animals, and the 25kg of meat the two lions, Zing Zong and Dolly, eat every day. Zookeeper Aziz Ahmad is also an obliging guide with gruesome stories about the fate of the zoo's last elephant (the elephant house is completely destroyed) and for a small tip will show you the final resting place of the zoo's most famous resident, Marjan, the one-eyed lion. Donatella, the famous bear, is undergoing daily treatment for a nose infection from German ISAF. The zoo is open from 06.00–18.00 every day and entry costs 5AFA.

Babur Gardens

Mark our words! Located on Sarak-e-Chilsitun road, these six hectares of walled gardens are going to be one of the most beautiful spots in the city. After more than two decades of conflict, which saw the rival factions fire their rockets either over or into this former imperial park, the place was little more than a wasteland. However, today more than 20 gardeners toil away at the site, landscaping and planting. Already, new shrubs and the layout for a rose garden are visible. Trees and flowerbeds are also being planted. The gardens were built in the mid-16th century at the behest of the first Mogul emperor, Zahir-ed-Din Mohammad Babur Shah, great-grandson of Tamerlane, and remain one of the few cultural landscapes in Afghanistan to retain their original shape.

The entrance to the gardens is from the Sarak-e-Chilsitun main road that runs in front of the mountain. The gardens start out as a gentle climb up the mountainside. The last stretch is steeper, but it is worth going all the way up. Tucked away on the final terrace at the top is the tomb of the former king himself, Babur Shah. His wife

What to see

is buried separately, but her tombstone is possibly even more beautifully carved than that of her husband. Just below them is a wonderful little marble mosque built by Babur's successor, Shah Jahan, also dating from the mid-16th century. A restaurant is being built towards the top end of the gardens with a breathtaking view over Kabul below and the mountains beyond.

Though the garden is currently under construction, the director is confident that it will be finished for the summer of 2003. Despite their poor state, the gardens serve as a much-needed respite to the inhabitants of Kabul who come on Fridays (the Muslim equivalent of the Christian Sunday) to picnic and relax in relative calm. If you get a chance, make sure you put your head around the door of the large greenhouse in the far left-hand corner of the gardens as you look up the mountain. It is locked, so you will need to find the head gardener, but once inside you are in for a treat. It is packed with colourful flowers and shrubs awaiting transplantation. One look in here and you know it is only a matter of time before Babur is returned to its former glory. Open every day 07.00–19.00. Entrance 2AFA.

Bala Hissar

The ancient citadel and home of some of Afghanistan's most important kings is now off limits and extremely dangerous owing to unexploded bombs and landmines. However, this magnificent building, dating in parts, it is believed, from the 5th century, has played a role in every twist and turn in the city's often violent history.

Bala Hissar sits to the south of the modern city centre down to the right of Jad-i-Maiwand in Karte Naw. The famous Walls of Kabul, which are a staggering 20 feet high and 12 feet thick, start at the natural fortress and follow the mountain ridge in a sweeping curve down to the river.

Bala Hissar was originally divided into two parts: the lower fortress, where the stables, barracks and three royal palaces were contained; and the upper fortress, called Bala Hissar, which housed the armoury and was the home of the infamous Black Pit, the dungeon of Kabul. However, the arrival of the British in Kabul marked the end of the citadel. From 1839 onwards the British used it on and off as their barracks until the massacre of the British Mission by mutinous Afghan troops in 1879. General Roberts was dispatched to Kabul to quell the situation and took the citadel. Shortly afterwards, an explosion in the powder magazine partly destroyed upper Bala Hissar. General Roberts decided to finish the job off and ordered the destruction of the rest.

However, perhaps the last word lies with the founder of the Mogul Empire, the Emperor Babur, who captured the fort at the start of his conquering career and went on to write of the magnificent building: 'The citadel is of surprising height, and enjoys an excellent climate, overlooking the large lake, and three meadows which present a very beautiful prospect when the plains are green.' The area surrounding Bala Hissar is heavily mined and full of UXO though the fortress is home to the 55th Division. The big green gates are adorned with photos of Karzai and Massoud. Visitors are not allowed in.

What to see

Shah-do-Shamshira mosque

This beautiful square building on the Kabul River opposite the Pul-I-Shah-do-Shamshira Bridge is the Mosque of the King of Two Swords. According to legend, the mosque takes its name from a 7th-century battle that took place between attacking Islamic troops and defending Hindus. Despite fighting heroically with a sword in each hand, one of the Muslim head commanders fell in battle. It is his memory that is honoured by the mosque today. The two-storey edifice was built in the 1920s on the order of King Amanullah's mother on the site of one of Kabul's first mosques.

The building has seen better days. Bullet holes can be seen in the façade, but the doors are still open to worshippers and visitors alike. Women are advised to visit on Wednesdays when the mosque is closed to men.

The National Gallery

Reconstruction and painting is being carried out at the National Gallery and it should be open soon. The gallery used to have some 820 paintings and portraits but 50% have been looted or destroyed; the director said the Taliban destroyed 210 portraits. Most of the collection is of European and Afghan landscapes and portraits of famous Afghan writers and kings, as well as a portrait of the French writer Victor Hugo.

The National Archive

Salang Wat Street; tel: 070 29 7805. Open every day 08.00–17.00 except Fridays. President Karzai reopened the National Archive in March 2002. There are some

15,000 documents and books but only photocopies are displayed in the two exhibition rooms. The originals are housed in a secret location, but written permission from the Ministry of Information and Culture will allow you to see the documents. The most famous exhibit in the collection is a 300-year-old copy of the Koran. One exhibition room houses poetry and writings by famous Afghan authors; the second room houses historical documents, newspapers and photographs including the 1919 independence from Britain agreement and old Afghan currency.

Perhaps one of the most striking things about the National Archive is the building itself. Emir Abdurrahman Khan built this beautiful 100-year-old mini palace for his son. The building reverted to the state on the Emir's death. The archive is still active. Every day new publications are stored for posterity. Official government documents, however, are only available for public viewing 40 years after the date of publication.

Royal Family Mausoleum

King Nadir Shah's Mausoleum is the resting place for the recent monarchs of Afghanistan's royal family. King Zahir Shah returned to Kabul in April 2002 after 29 years in exile. King Zahir's wife, Queen Homaira, never made it back to her homeland. She died in Italy at the age of 86 while waiting to rejoin her husband in Kabul and is now buried here. The queen is survived by seven of her nine children and by 14 grandchildren. Usually there's a man on duty at the mausoleum who will take you into the catacombs. There are good views of the city from here, giving you an idea of how the infighting Mujaheddin fought over the high ground and destroyed the city from it.

OMAR Mine Museum

The OMAR Mines and UXOs Museum on Street 13 in Wazir Akbar Khan (tel: 020 210 0833; email: omarintl@ceretechs.com) has a collection of 51 types of mines out of the 53 used in Afghanistan over the years, including cluster bombs and air-drop bombs used by the US in 2002. OMAR stands for Organisation for Mine Clearance and Afghan Rehabilitation. Unfortunately, the museum is not really open for casual visitors who just turn up. You need to go the main OMAR office on Street 10, House 206 in Wazir Akbar Khan and try to organise a time to visit. A typical tour round the garden and display cases will take around 45 minutes. Ask for Dr Shah Walie who knows everything there is to know about mines.

Bibi Mahro Hill

Take a walk up the Bibi Mahro Hill behind Wazir Akbar Khan for some superb views of Kabul city, especially at sunset. There's a former Soviet Olympic-size swimming pool at the top of the hill and old trenches and armoured personnel carriers. Many of the expatriates living in Wazir Akbar Khan below use the short climb to the top of the hill as their daily exercise routine and you may even see a few joggers. The area has been cleared of mines but still take the necessary precautions. Despite the relative acceptance of foreigners here, women should never go unaccompanied.

There have been isolated incidents of stone-throwing here by the youths who linger around the top of the hill.

Christian cemetery

Char-i-Shahid, Shahre Naw. Open every day 07.00–16.00. This walled graveyard of around 150 graves is behind large arched wooden doors about 150m beyond the martyr's shrine on Char-i-Shahid. Christians have been buried here for more than 100 years. The most famous grave is that of the scholar, author and explorer, Mark Aurel Stein of the Indian Archaeological Survey. He was born in Budapest in 1862 and died in Kabul in October 1943. His simple tombstone alludes to his travels throughout Asia and his contribution to the West's understanding of the region. More recent additions to the cemetery are the ISAF memorial plaques. As you walk in, to the right, there is one to the British soldiers and officers who died in the Afghan wars in the 19th and 20th centuries, which was placed in the wall in 2002. Opposite, at the other end, there is a memorial plaque to the German soldiers and officers who lost their lives in Afghanistan, placed by German ISAF. Other plaques to ISAF soldiers can also be spotted in the perimeter walls. Around 50 people visit the graveyard every week.

Other things to see

There are plenty of places to discover in Kabul, depending on your interests and how you feel about being followed around everywhere you go.

Certainly visit the **money market**. Experience the stomach-churning thrill of

What to see

THE CEMETERY GUARDIAN

Sixty-year-old Rahim Mullah has been tending the graves at the Christian cemetery for 17 years and can give lots of extra insights into the history of those buried here. For Rahim, the Taliban period was a difficult one. He confesses that he was heavily criticised during that time for continuing to tend the cemetery. And though he was salaried, his income dried up after the NGO who was paying him, the International Organisation for Migration, was bombed and pulled out of the country. Money was sent in from Peshawar in Pakistan, but it was an uncertain trickle of funds. He was even confronted by Mullah Omar three months before the fall of the Taliban in November 2001. The Taliban headquarters were in the buildings that line the right wall of the cemetery as you enter. One day, the famed, one-eyed leader of the Taliban decided to see the graveyard for himself. He was shown around by Rahim and stayed for 20 minutes. But before leaving Mullah Omar asked Rahim what he thought he was doing working in such a place. 'I am an illiterate man,' answered Rahim, 'and everyone knows that to be illiterate is like being blind (and therefore ignorant).' To which Mullah Omar is reputed to have replied, 'But I too am blind!' before clapping Rahim on the back and bursting into laughter. Today the British Embassy in Kabul pays Rahim's salary and he looks forward to passing the mantle of service on to his eldest son.

Kabul City

seeing garrulous old men spirit away your hard-earned hard currency and present you with a bundle of unknown notes. Despite the distinctly non-high-tech setting, the money dealers have all the latest exchange rates at their fingertips (they were the first people in Kabul to get satellite phones), and it is no problem to change dollars, pounds sterling, euros and Pakistani rupees.

Then there's the **Titanic market** in the dried up Kabul River. It gets its name from the blockbuster Hollywood movie *Titanic*: when the river occasionally floods, the market sinks! This is the place for plastic soap dishes and factory-produced carpets from Iran.

You can buy any type of bird in the noisy **Ka Farushi bird market** near the Blue Mosque in the old city across the main bridge over Kabul River.

The **Ariana Graveyard**, as the collection of circa 1960–85 trashed aviation memorabilia is called, will probably be the first thing you see on arrival in Kabul. The rusting heap of vintage planes lies to the right of the airport as you head into the city. Much of it is the result of coalition attacks in 2001, though the real damage was done between 1991 and 1996 when rival Mujaheddin factions battled for control of the city. Gulbuddin Hekmatyar, the leader of Hezb-i-Islami (Islamic Party) launched constant attacks on the airport right up until the Taliban take-over of the city.

EXCURSIONS BEYOND KABUL
Paghman Gardens
King Amanullah brought in foreign experts to redesign the Paghman district after his tour of Europe, India and Iran in 1927–28. The small village of Paghman at the bottom

DAY TRIP OUT OF KABUL: SHOMALI PLAIN AND THE ARTISAN'S VILLAGE, ISTALIF

This village, 50-minutes' drive out of Kabul, is a terrible reminder of the devastation caused by the bitter war fought for the area by the Taliban and the Northern Alliance. Today it is mostly in ruins, but a small artisan initiative is breathing tentative life into the place. The small number of craftsmen consists mostly of potters and their creations have a compelling rustic beauty. The colours they use are mostly royal blue and deep turquoise. The merchandise ranges from salad bowls and plates to jugs and teacups and saucers.

To reach Istalif head out of Kabul on the Shomali road. After 45 minutes you will pass a white roadside petrol pump on the left and see immediately a turning to the left marked by NGO signposts. This dirt road leads up into the foothills of the mountains that fringe the Shomali Plain. Follow the road for about 20 minutes. As you ascend, you will come across a sharp hairpin bend. Shortly afterwards, as you continue along the road, you will reach the brow of

of the Hindu Kush became a holiday retreat with villas and chalets and an 'Arc de Triomphe' style arch. The gardens were beautifully laid out and copied from European designs. But as with West Kabul and the elaborate Darulaman Palace area (built, incidentally, by the same French and German architects), Paghman became a

the small hill you are climbing. Bear left at the intersection here and descend into a valley with a beautiful river at the bottom. On the other side of the river is Istalif.

The first thing you will come across as you enter the village is the *chai kana* or teahouse. This is a good place for some biscuits, *naan*, green tea and gossip. This bit of the village is fairly intact, but continue up through the village and you will find devastated streets and derelict buildings just behind. On the old (now destroyed) main thoroughfare you will find the outlet for the local pottery made in Istalif. An old man is happy to let you browse and will explain the local history for those with enough Dari to understand him. He is a keen businessman and you should haggle for any purchases you intend to make, though once you've seen the ruins the people of Istalif live in, it feels right to pay a little over the odds. At the top of the village is the mosque and some large trees. The view of the plain is wonderful from here. As long as prayers are not going on, you are allowed to sit in the shade and contemplate the scene laid out before you.

Mujaheddin battleground. Today, little is left, though the arch still stands. Nevertheless, in the summer this remains popular for picnics and days out of the city. It is approximately 45 minutes' drive.

Excursions beyond Kabul

Further afield

Make special efforts to find a good and reliable driver who knows the road and the area for all your trips out of Kabul. Afghans will often go to the **Kargha Dam** outside the city in the summer for picnics.

Another place worth visiting is the breathtaking **Kabul River Gorge**, probably one of the most majestic in the world.

Outside Kabul, you should also consider a trip to **Bamyian** to see the destroyed Buddhas. A road journey will take you some eight hours, though a plane journey with UNHAS will take you only 20 minutes. A day trip to **Ghazni** to see the spectacular minarets is possible but it will take you about four hours to get there and a 4WD is essential for the 130km journey on asvery bad road. Just take care walking around the two minarets: Ghazni has been heavily fought for over the years. Just take care walking around the two minarets as Ghazni has been heavily fought for over the years and the area is likely to contain some unexploded shells.

A day trip to **Gardez** is also possible. There's not a lot in Gardez itself but the 2½–3-hour-drive there, along a very good tarmac road, takes you through spectacular desert and amazing mountainous ranges, with nomads and their camels along the route. Be sure to check the security situation before heading out.

The Panjshir Valley

The Panjshir Valley lies around 100km northeast of Kabul, but the journey there takes more than five hours. The first 50km are tarmacked road, but suddenly the road ends and after that it's just rocks and dust, making the ride rather uncomfortable.

Head out of Kabul towards Charikar (a good place to stop and eat at the Panjshir Restaurant on the main town square). Dozens of burnt-out tanks still line the road, testimonies to the violent fighting that raged in the region as the Soviets battled to subdue the Panjshir and repeatedly failed.

Massoud's tomb is a plain white building with a gleaming green dome towards the valley entrance. The pilgrimage site, as it has now become, is perched on a hill with a commanding and beautiful view of the river far below. The Panjshir River is one of the few fast-flowing rivers in the country after five years of drought and the valley floor is a scene of biblical lushness, especially around harvest time in September (also the time of the anniversary of Massoud's death). Plans are afoot to expand the tomb and make it into a national monument.

When visiting be careful not to offend others. Women should wear scarves, and both men and women should remove shoes if they wish to enter the small tomb itself.

1

LANGUAGE

Pashto and Dari (Afghan Persian) both belong to the Indo-European language group. Dari, however, is a west Iranian language derived from Farsi (the language spoken in Iran), while Pashto is east Iranian in origin. It's thought that the two language systems started to diverge several centuries BC. Both are written in Arabic script, and have many Arabic and Iranian 'loan' words.

Dari has eight vowels and a set of consonants quite similar to those of English. Generally, the stress falls on the last syllable of the word. Pashto has seven vowels, and generally the same consonants as Dari does, but in addition has a series of retroflex consonants: *t, d, r, n,* and in the Kandahar dialect *sh*. Retroflex consonants (the English r is a retroflex) are made by curling the tongue backward.

Pashto distinguishes between two grammatical genders as well as singular and plural. Verbs agree with their subjects in person, number, and grammatical gender as well as being marked for tense. Word order in sentences for both Dari and Pashto is subject-object-verb. Dari nouns have no grammatical gender, but are marked for person and number (singular and plural).

Dari and Pashto phrasebook

	Dari	*Pashto*
How are you?	*Chi-toor-hasty*	*Senga ye?*
I am fine	*Khub-os-tom*	*Zek Kha yom*
Thank you	*Ta-shar-koor*	*Manena*

	Dari	**Pashto**
Goodbye	*Khuda Hafiz*	*De khudai paman*
My name is …	*Nam man …*	*Zema num … dai*
What is your name?	*Nama-shuma cheast?*	*Stanum sedai?*
left	*chap*	*kheen*
right	*rost*	*khee*
straight	*rubaru*	*makhamokh*
back	*posht* or *akib*	*sha khwa*
Monday	*Dushanbe*	*Doshanba*
Tuesday	*Seshanbe*	*Seshanba*
Wednesday	*Charshanbe*	*Charshanba*
Thursday	*Panjshanbe*	*Panjshanba*
Friday	*Juma*	*Juma*
Saturday	*Shanbe*	*Shanba*
Sunday	*Yakshanbe*	*Yakshanba*
1	*yak*	*yawa*
2	*du*	*dua*
3	*say*	*dre*
4	*char*	*salor*

Language

	Dari	*Pashto*
5	*panj*	*penza*
6	*shash*	*shpag*
7	*aft*	*owa*
8	*asht*	*ata*
9	*nu*	*nah*
10	*da*	*las*
11	*yaazdah*	*yawa las*
12	*duaazdah*	*dua las*
o'clock	*baja*	*baja*
I am going	*Man merawam*	*Ze zom*
I'm sorry	*Bubakhshen*	*Wo bakhe*
yesterday	*diroz*	*paroon*
today	*emroz*	*nen*
tomorrow	*farda*	*saba*
every day	*harroz*	*hara wroz*
crazy	*dewana*	*lewanai*
once again	*yak dafa digar*	*yaw zel bya*

Appendix I

NGOS AND INTERNATIONAL ORGANISATIONS IN KABUL

An invaluable source of information is *The A to Z Guide to Afghanistan Assistance* produced in August 2002 by the Afghanistan Research and Evaluation Unit (AREU, Prime Minister's Compound, next to AACA; tel: 070 27 6637; web: www.areu.org.pk). The book contains maps, documents and list of organisations working in Afghanistan. Many of the contact names from August 2002 are now out of date but an updated book is planned for 2003.

Major donors
DFID (UK Department for International Development) www.dfid.gov.uk
European Union www.europa.eu.int
Japan ODA (Official Development Assistance) www.mofa.go.jp
USAID (United States Agency for International Development) www.usaid.gov
WORLD BANK www.worldbank.org

UN agencies
United Nations Assistance Mission in Afghanistan (UNAMA, formerly UNSMA special mission) www.unama-afg.org
United Nations Development Programme (UNDP) www.undp.org
United Nations Educational, Scientific and Cultural Organisation (UNESCO) www.unesco.org
United Nations High Commissioner for Refugees (UNHCR) www.unhcr.ch
United Nations Children's Fund (UNICEF) www.unicef.org

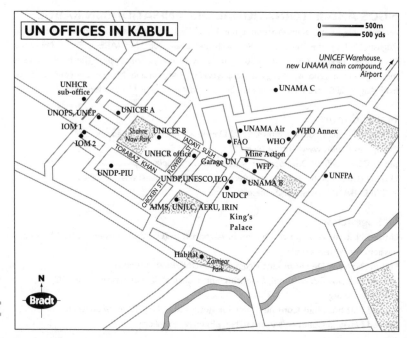

UN OFFICES IN KABUL

0 — 500m
0 — 500 yds

*UNICEF Warehouse,
new UNAMA main compound,
Airport*

UNHCR
sub-office

UNOPS, UNEP

IOM 1

IOM 2

UNICEF A

*Shahre
Naw Park*

UNICEF B

JADAYI SULH

TORABAZ KHAN

UNHCR office

FLOWER ST

UNDP-PIU

CHICKEN ST

UNDP, UNESCO, ILO

AIMS, UNJLC, AERU, IRIN

UNAMA C

UNAMA Air

WHO Annex

FAO

WHO

Mine Action

Garage UN

WFP

UNAMA B

UNFPA

UNDCP

King's
Palace

Habitat

*Zarnigar
Park*

N

Bradt

United Nations Development Fund for Women (UNIFEM) www.undp.org/unifem
United Nations Office for the Coordination of Humanitarian Affairs (UNOCHA)
www.reliefweb.int/ocha_ol
World Food Programme (WFP) www.wfp.org
World Health Organisation (WHO) www.who.int

Non-profit organisations implementing aid programmes in Afghanistan

(source USAID – www.usaid.gov)

Action Against Hunger	www.aah-usa.org
ADRA International	www.adra.org
American Friends Service Committee (AFSC)	www.afsc.org
American Jewish World Service	www.ajws.org
American Refugee Committee	www.archq.org
AmeriCares Foundation	www.americares.org
CARE	www.care.org
Carelift International	www.carelift.org
Catholic Relief Services	www.catholicrelief.org
CHF International	www.chfhq.org
Childreach/Plan International USA	www.childreach.org
Christian Children's Fund	www.christianchildrensfund.org
Christian Reformed World Relief Committee	www.crwrc.org

NGOs

Appendix 2

Church World Service	www.churchworldservice.org
Concern Worldwide US	www.concernusa.org
Direct Relief International	www.directrelief.org
Doctors of the World	www.doctorsoftheworld.org
Doctors Without Borders/ Médecins Sans Frontières (MSF)	www.doctorswithoutborders.org
Food for the Hungry, Inc	www.fh.org
International Aid	www.internationalaid.org
International Catholic Migration Commission	www.icmc.net
HOPE Worldwide	www.hopeworldwide.org
International Medical Corps	www.imc-la.org
International Rescue Committee	www.theirc.org
Lutheran World Relief	www.lwr.org
MAP International	www.map.org
Mercy Corps	www.mercycorps.org
Northwest Medical Teams	www.nwmedicalteams.org
Operation USA	www.opusa.org
Oxfam America	www.oxfamamerica.org
Refugees International	wwwrefugeesinternational.org
Relief International	www.ri.org
Salvation Army World Service Office	www.salvationarmyusa.org
Samaritan's Purse	www.samaritan.org

Save the Children	www.savethechildren.org
United Methodist Committee On Relief	www.gbgm-umc.org/umcor
USA for UNHCR	www.usaforunhcr.org
United States Fund for UNICEF	www.unicefusa.org
United Way International	www.uwint.org
World Concern	www.worldconcern.org
World Food Programme	www.wfp.org
World Relief	www.worldrelief.org
World Vision	www.worldvision.org

Others

Action Contre La Faim (Action Against Hunger, ACF) www.acf-fr.org; www.aah-usa.org; www.aahuk.org

ACTIONAID www.actionaid.org

MSF www.msf.org

Caritas Internationalis www.caritas-network-for-afghanistan.org A confederation of 154 Catholic relief, development and social service organisations present in 198 countries and territories

The International Committee of the Red Cross (ICRC) www.icrc.org

International Federation of Red Cross and Red Crescent Societies (IFRC) www.ifrc.org

International Organisation On Migration (IOM) www.iom.org

NGOs

IOM Return of Qualified Afghans (The International Organisation on Migration) www.iom-rqa.org Details of the IOM programme to encourage Afghans to return home; includes interesting profiles of Afghans who have returned.

Oxford Committee for Famine Relief www.oxfam.org.uk

Media development

AINA www.ainaworld.org. AINA set up the highly popular Media and Cultural Centre next door to the Ministry of Planning. A number of media development NGOs and Afghan media groups base themselves here. Meetings, exhibitions, film showings and talks are held regularly.

Baltic Media Centre www.bmc.dk. With EC funding the Baltic Media Centre helped Radio Afghanistan start two radio programmes, 'Good Morning Afghanistan' and 'Good Evening Afghanistan'.

BBC World Service Trust www.bbc.co.uk/worldservice/us/trust. The BBC began a series of training courses in early 2002 along with support for Radio Afghanistan. With funding from DFID two digital studios were installed at Radio Afghanistan and transmitters donated. The BBC World Service is also available in Kabul on 89.0FM.

IMPACS (the Institute for Media, Policy and Civil Society) www.impacs.org. Funded by Canada, IMPACS is helping community radio stations to develop in Afghanistan and developing the role of women in the media.

Institute for War and Peace Reporting www.iwpr.net. IWPR is carrying out journalism training and stories by Afghan journalists are published by IWPR.

International Media Support www.i-m-s.dk. Danish media NGO.

Internews www.internews.org. In 2002 Internews launched a USAID-funded project of journalism training as well as organising donations of broadcasting equipment to radio stations. Internews also administers Ahmed Rashid's Open Media Fund for Afghanistan that awards grants to Afghan media groups.

RFE/RL www.rferl.org. Radio Free Afghanistan, which is part of Radio Free Europe and Radio Liberty, has an Afghan journalists training programme offering courses in Kabul and the chance for Afghan journalists to visit the USA.

Media Action International www.mediaaction.org. MAI is carrying out journalism training, especially at the universities; MAI also publishes the Crosslines Afghanistan Monitor.

NGOs

3 GOVERNMENT MINISTRIES AND MINISTERS
Islamic Transitional State of Afghanistan (web: www.af)
President
Hamid Karzai

Vice-presidents
Abdul Karim Khalili
Mohammed Qaseem Fahim
Hedayat Armin Arsala
Ustad Nematollah Shahrani

The cabinet

Agriculture	Sayed Hussain Anwari
Borders and Tribal Affairs	Mohammed Arif Nurzai
Civil Aviation and Tourism	Mir Wais Saddiq (son of Herat Governor Ismail Khan)
Commerce	Sayed Mustafa Kasemi
Communications	Mohammad Masoom Stanakzai (web: www.af-com-ministry.org)
Defence	Mohammed Qaseem Fahim
Education	Yunus Qanooni
Finance	Dr Ashraf Ghani Ahmadzai
Foreign	Dr Abdullah Abdullah

Haj and Mosques	Mohammed Amin Naziryar
Higher Education	Sherief Fayez
Information and Culture	Dr Sayed Makhdoom Raheen
Interior	Ali Ahmad Jalali
Irrigation and Environment	Ahmed Yusuf Nooristani
Justice	Abbas Karimi
Light Industry	Mohammed Alim Razm
Martyrs and Disabled	Abdullah Wardak
Minister of State for Women's Affairs	Mahbooba Huquqmal
Planning	Mohammed Mohaqik
Public Health	Dr Sohaila Siddiqi
Public Works	Engineer Ali
Reconstruction	Mohammed Amin Farhang
Refugees	Intayatullah Nazeri
Rural Development	Hanif Atmar
Social Affairs	Noor Mohammed Karkin
Supreme Court Chief Justice	Sheikh Fazl Hadi Shinwari
Transportation	Saeed Mohammed Ali Jawad
Urban Affairs	Yusuf Pashtun
Water and Power	Ahmed Shakar Kargar
Women's Affairs	Habiba Sorabi

Government ministries

4

FURTHER READING
Books

Here is a list of some books read by the authors and recommended by friends. Bookshops in Kabul stock recent books on Afghanistan and out-of-date editions such as those by Nancy Hatch Dupree.

The most recent bestseller and 'must-read' on Afghanistan is Ahmed Rashid's *Taliban: The Story of the Afghan Warlords* (Pan Books, 2001)

An essential handbook with a new edition due out soon: Edward Girardet and Jonathan Walker (eds) *Afghanistan – Essential Field Guides to Humanitarian and Conflict Zones*. Originally published in 1998 a revised edition is due out in 2003. This is a handbook anyone visiting Afghanistan should not be without.

Look out on the streets of Kabul for *An Historical Guide to Afghanistan* (1977) and *An Historical Guide to Kabul* (1972) both by Nancy Hatch Dupree.

Other books worth reading include:

Allen, Charles *Soldier Sahibs: The Men who Made the North-West Frontier* (Abacus, 2001)

Anderson, Jon Lee *The Lion's Grave: Dispatches from Afghanistan* (Grove Press, Atlantic, 2002)

Babur, the Emperor *The Baburnama, Memoirs of Babur Prince and Emperor* (The Modern Library Classics, 2002)

Borovik, Artyom *The Hidden War: A Russian Journalist's Account of the Soviet War in Afghanistan* (Groove Press, 2001)

Danziger, Nick *Danziger's Travels: Beyond Forbidden Frontiers* (Flamingo, 1993)

Dupree, Louis *Afghanistan* (Princeton University Press, 1980)

Elliot, Jason *An Unexpected Light: Travels in Afghanistan* (Picador, 2000)

Ewans, Martin *Afghanistan, A Short History of its People and Politics* (Perennial, 2002)

Griffiths, John C *Afghanistan, A History of Conflict* (André Deutsch Ltd, 2001)

Hopkirk, Peter *The Great Game: On Secret Service in High Asia* (Oxford University Press, 2001)

Hopkirk, Peter *The Great Game: The Struggle for Empire in Central Asia* (Kodansha America, 1994)

Kaplan, Robert D *Soldiers of God: With the Mujahidin in Afghanistan* (Houghton Mifflin Co, 1990)

Lamb, Christina *The Sewing Circles of Herat: My Afghan Years* (Harper Collins, 2002)

Levi, Peter *The Light Garden of the Angel King, Travels in Afghanistan with Bruce Chatwin* (Pallas Athene, 2002)

Newby, Eric *A Short Walk in the Hindu Kush* (Picador, 1981)

Rall, Ted *To Afghanistan and Back* (NBM Publishing Company, 2002)

Rashid, Ahmed *Jihad: The Rise of Militant Islam in Central Asia* (Yale University Press, 2002)

Reuter's Foreign Correspondents *Afghanistan: Lifting the Veil* (Prentice Hall, 2002)

Rubin, Barnett R *The Fragmentation of Afghanistan: State Formation and Collapse in the International System* (Yale University Press, 2002)

Rubin, Barnett R *The Search for Peace in Afghanistan: From Buffer State to Failed State* (Yale University Press, 1995)

Further reading

Siba, Shakib *Afghanistan, Where God only Comes to Weep* (Century, 2001)

Simpson, John *News from No Man's Land: Reporting the World* (Macmillan, 2002)

Tanner, Stephen *Afghanistan, A Military History from Alexander the Great to the Fall of the Taliban* (Da Capo Press, 2002)

Tarn, WW *The Greeks in Bactria and India* (Ares Publishers, 1997)

Zoya et al *Zoya's Story: A Woman's Struggle for Freedom in Afghanistan* (Review, 2003)

For a critical analysis of the work of NGOs worldwide read David Rieff's *A Bed for the Night: Humanitarianism in Crisis* (Vintage, 2002)

Websites

There are a number of websites, too numerous to list here, related to Afghanistan on the worldwide web, not just from official groups but also from Afghan exiles. Below is just a selection of the most interesting, informative and popular ones.

News and information

AIMS www.aims.org.pk. Afghanistan Information Management Service provides maps and information for the whole country.

BAAG (British Agencies Afghanistan Group) www.baag.org.uk. BAAG was set up by British NGOs in 1987 as an umbrella group to draw public attention to the humanitarian needs of the population of Afghanistan and of Afghan refugees in Iran and Pakistan. Good (online, and by email) monthly briefing material for those working in Afghanistan.

Appendix 4

BBC www.bbc.co.uk. The main BBC website is a good place to start surfing around. Check out the South Asia news pages for the latest from Afghanistan, the BBC profile of Afghanistan, the latest weather forecast for Kabul and the special sections on the Fall of Kabul and the War on Terror. The 'From Our Own Correspondent' pages also feature articles on Kabul and Afghanistan.

CNN www.cnn.com. News from CNN including special reports on the War on Terror.

Eurasianet www.eurasianet.org. An excellent source of news and background information on Afghanistan from the Open Society Institute in New York. Eurasianet offers information and analysis on Central Asia and the Caucasus.

Human Rights Watch www.hrw.org/asia/afghanistan.php. Reports, briefings and press releases from Human Rights Watch on issues in Afghanistan such as the treatment of women and the use of cluster bombs. There's also an analysis on conditions in Afghanistan one year after the December 2001 Bonn Agreement.

International Crisis Group www.crisisweb.org. Detailed reports and analysis from the ICG which specialises in reporting on and investigating transitional countries. Reports on Afghanistan include judicial reform and transitional justice and a briefing on the Transitional Administration.

IWPR www.iwpr.net. The Institute for War and Peace Reporting has an extensive page of news from Afghanistan and a profile and map of the country. IWPR has been conducting journalism training in Afghanistan. Afghan journalists contribute news to the IWPR website and publications as part of their training.

IRIN News Agency www.irinnews.org. Compiled by the United Nations IRIN (Integrated

Regional Information Networks) is a good source of daily news from Afghanistan and other crisis- and disaster-affected countries where the UN is operating. You can also subscribe to regular email news from IRIN.

National Geographic www.nationalgeographic.com/landincrisis. Great maps, news and photographs from *National Geographic* including the search for the famous Afghan Girl.

The Crosslines Afghanistan Monitor www.afghanmonitor.org. Produced by long-time Afghanistan journalist Eddie Girardet and Media Action International examining reconstruction and peacekeeping operations in Afghanistan.

The Guardian www.guardian.co.uk/afghanistan. The *Guardian* has an extensive special report website on Afghanistan featuring interactive guides, comment and analysis, and coverage on issues such as life in Afghanistan, reconstruction, NATO, security, and the Taliban.

United Nations www.un.org. All UN agencies working in Afghanistan have extensive web pages with the latest details on their activities. The **United Nations Assistance Mission in Afghanistan** (UNAMA, formerly Special Mission UNSMA) is online at www.unama-afg.org. Check at the UN News Centre for transcripts of the press conferences in Kabul and other details on the peace process in Afghanistan. **UNESCO** (www.unesco.org/afghanistan) has detailed information on its projects especially on the fight to save the archaeological and historical sites from illegal excavations. **UNICEF** (www.unicef.org/noteworthy/afghanistan) has information on its projects and the **UNHCR Return to Afghanistan** pages (www.unhcr.ch/cgi-bin/texis/vtx/afghan) have details on the huge refugee return programme since the fall of the Taliban. UN news sites also include **Reliefweb** (www.reliefweb.org) and the IRIN news agency (www.irinnews.org, see above).

A new website, **www.kabulcaravan.com**, also promises to be a good guide to Afghanistan.

News, features, articles, information and more on Afghanistan can be obtained from a number of websites, including:

Afghanistan Directory www.afghana.com.
Up to date news from www.afghannews.net
Afghan Daily www.afghandaily.com
Afghanistan Online www.afghan-web.com
Afghan News Channel www.afghan-network.net/news
Afghan Online www.afghanonline.com
E-Ariana.com www.e-ariana.com
yahoo.com in the full-coverage news section on Afghanistan.

The **US Public Affairs Program for Afghanistan** also features information on US activities in Afghanistan (www.usembassy.state.gov/afghanistan). The **CIA World Factbook** on Afghanistan contains a number of basic facts and figures (www.cia.gov/cia/publications/factbook/geos/af/html).

For information and advice on travel to Afghanistan check the **British Foreign and Commonwealth Travel Warning pages** (www.fco.gov.uk). American citizens might want to check the **US State Department** pages (www.travel.state.gov/Afghanistan.html) and for the latest travel warnings visit www.travel.state.gov/Afghanistan_warning/html.

Further reading

A couple of interesting websites include those by **Jake Sutton** (www.afghanistanportraits.com) a freelance cameraman and painter who spent much of 2002 in Afghanistan doing charcoal portraits of Afghans and visitors (see pages 134–5).

Khorshied Machalle Nusratty (www.forafghanistan.com and www.artistsforafghanistan.org) is an Afghan American from California who came to her father's country for the first time in 2002 and stayed. Khorshied has set up the Artists for Afghanistan Foundation to encourage the development of music and the arts. See also pages 48–9.

Some Afghans from Melbourne, Australia, compile a free daily digest of news on Afghanistan. To subscribe, email: info@mobycapital.com.

Updates for this book are being placed online at www.kabulguide.net.

Appendix 4

SELECTION OF BRADT TRAVEL GUIDES

Africa by Road
Albania
Amazon, The
Azores
Baltic Capitals: Tallinn, Riga,
    Vilnius, Kaliningrad
Belize
Botswana: Okavango, Chobe,
    Northern Kalahari
Cambodia
Canada: North
Cape Verde Islands
Cayman Islands
Chile and Argentina: Trekking
China: Yunnan Province
Croatia
Cuba
East and Southern Africa
Ecuador, Climbing and Hiking
    in
Ecuador, Peru and Bolivia
Eritrea

Estonia
Ethiopia
Falkland Islands
Gabon, São Tome & Principe
Gambia, The
Georgia
Ghana
Haiti and Dominican Republic
Iran
Iraq
Latvia
Lithuania
Madagascar
Malawi
Maldives
Mali
Mauritius, Rodrigues and
    Réunion
Mongolia
Montenegro
Mozambique
Namibia

North Cyprus
North Korea
Palestine, with Jerusalem
Peru and Bolivia: Trekking
Rwanda
St Helena, Ascension, Tristan
    da Cunha
Seychelles
Singapore
South Africa: Budget Travel
    Guide
Sri Lanka
Switzerland: Rail, Road, Lake
Tanzania
Tasmania
Tibet
Uganda
Ukraine
USA by Rail
Venezuela
Zambia
Zanzibar

Page numbers in **bold** indicate major entries;
those in *italics* indicate maps.

Index